EBERHARD WEBER

Popular Music History

Series Editor: Alyn Shipton, Royal Academy of Music, London.

This series publishes books that extend the field of popular music studies, examine the lives and careers of key musicians, interrogate histories of genres, focus on previously neglected forms, or engage in the formative history of popular music styles.

Published

An Unholy Row: Jazz in Britain and its Audience, 1945–1960
Dave Gelly

Being Prez: The Life and Music of Lester Young
Dave Gelly

Bill Russell and the New Orleans Jazz Revival
Ray Smith and Mike Pointon

Chasin' the Bird: The Life and Legacy of Charlie Parker
Brian Priestley

Handful of Keys: Conversations with Thirty Jazz Pianists
Alyn Shipton

Hear My Train A Comin': The Songs of Jimi Hendrix
Kevin Le Gendre

Jazz Me Blues: The Autobiography of Chris Barber
Chris Barber with Alyn Shipton

Jazz Visions: Lennie Tristano and His Legacy
Peter Ind

Keith Jarrett: A Biography
Wolfgang Sandner, translated by Chris Jarrett

Komeda: A Private Life in Jazz
Magdalena Grzebałkowska, translated by Halina Boniszewska

Lee Morgan: His Life, Music and Culture
Tom Perchard

Lionel Richie: Hello
Sharon Davis

Mosaics: The Life and Works of Graham Collier
Duncan Heining

Mr P.C.: The Life and Music of Paul Chambers
Rob Palmer

Out of the Long Dark: The Life of Ian Carr
Alyn Shipton

Rufus Wainwright
Katherine Williams

Scouse Pop
Paul Skillen

Soul Unsung: Reflections on the Band in Black Popular Music
Kevin Le Gendre

The Godfather of British Jazz: The Life and Music of Stan Tracey
Clark Tracey

The History of European Jazz: The Music, Musicians and Audience in Context
Edited by Francesco Martinelli

The Last Miles: The Music of Miles Davis, 1980–1991
George Cole

The Long Shadow of the Little Giant (second edition): The Life, Work and Legacy of Tubby Hayes
Simon Spillett

The Ultimate Guide to Great Reggae: The Complete Story of Reggae Told through its Greatest Songs, Famous and Forgotten
Michael Garnice

This is Bop: Jon Hendricks and the Art of Vocal Jazz
Peter Jones

This is Hip: The Life of Mark Murphy
Peter Jones

Trad Dads, Dirty Boppers and Free Fusioneers: A History of British Jazz, 1960–1975
Duncan Heining

Two Bold Singermen and the English Folk Revival: The Lives, Song Traditions and Legacies of Sam Larner and Harry Cox
Bruce Lindsay

Vinyl Ventures: My Fifty Years at Rounder Records
Bill Nowlin

Eberhard Weber

A German Jazz Story

Eberhard Weber
Translated by Heidi Kirk

equinox

SHEFFIELD UK   BRISTOL CT

Published by Equinox Publishing Ltd

UK: Office 415, The Workstation, 15 Paternoster Row, Sheffield, South Yorkshire,
      S1 2BX
USA: ISD, 70 Enterprise Drive, Bristol, CT 06010

www.equinoxpub.com

The translation of this work was supported by a grant from the Goethe-Institut.

First published in German as *Eberhard Weber Résumé: Eine Deutsche Jazz- Geschichte*
by sagas.edition Stuttgart 2015.
This first English edition published by Equinox Publishing Ltd 2021.

British Library Cataloguing-in-Publication Data

A catalogue record for this book is available from the British Library.

ISBN-13 978 1 80050 082 2   (hardback)
         978 1 80050 083 9   (ePDF)
         978 1 80050 116 4   (ePub)

Library of Congress Cataloging-in-Publication Data

Names: Weber, Eberhard, 1940- author. | Kirk, Heidi, translator.
Title: Eberhard Weber : a German jazz story / Eberhard Weber ; translated
   by Heidi Kirk.
Other titles: Résumé. English
Description: First English edition. | Bristol : Equinox Publishing Ltd,
   2021. | Series: Popular music history | Includes index. | Summary:
   "Eberhard Weber is a virtuoso who revolutionized jazz bass playing. His
   remarkable autobiography is at the same time a humorous and exciting
   testimony to a vital period in German jazz history. This is the first
   English translation of the original published in German by sagas.edition Stuttgart
   2015"-- Provided by publisher.
Identifiers: LCCN 2021012912 (print) | LCCN 2021012913 (ebook) | ISBN
   9781800500822 (hardback) | ISBN 9781800500839 (pdf) | ISBN 9781800501164
   (epub)
Subjects: LCSH: Weber, Eberhard, 1940- | Jazz
   musicians--Germany--Biography. | Double bassists--Germany--Biography. |
   LCGFT: Autobiographies.
Classification: LCC ML418.W29 A3 2021 (print) | LCC ML418.W29 (ebook) |
   DDC 787.5092 [B]--dc23
LC record available at https://lccn.loc.gov/2021012912
LC ebook record available at https://lccn.loc.gov/2021012913

Typeset by S.J.I. Services, New Delhi, India

Contents

Prelude vii

1 A Stroke of Bad Luck 1

2 If Only I Knew 9

3 Under the Grand Piano 17

4 "A dab hand" 33

5 "Hey, how about it?" 46

6 Free!? 61

7 Telephone Bass Player 71

8 "I'm gonna get myself one!" 78

9 New Colours 91

10 Philharmonic Full Circle 100

11 Well Received 102

12 "Now you've made it!" 112

13 Down Under 118

14 Longer than Most Marriages 125

15 United (Kingdom) 130

16 Border Crossings 140

17 Highs and Lows 146

18	To Poona, Please!	149
19	Home Advantage?	157
20	Perfect Sound	158
	Postlude	167
	Discography	171
	Index	178

Prelude

My name is Eberhard Weber, but then, you already know that. After all, it's written on the cover. Possibly that's even why you purchased the book. For a solid forty years, I was in the jazz business – professionally from 1973, and as an amateur before that, from about 1962. You probably know that, too. In 2007 I was forced to give up my active career as a bass player because I haven't been physically able to coax decent sounds out of my instrument since then. You know that, too? You see, this is where the problem starts. I don't exactly want to rehash what has already been repeated ad nauseam in so many publications.

That's why, when I first started contemplating writing a book, I asked myself what should be included and what not. Now, at the age of seventy-five, after fifty years of belonging to the scene, I often wonder: Why all this? Was it worth it? Has the music evolved? Does it have to? Who or what has curbed or hastened the pace of its development? Are these even criteria? Fifty years ago, I hardly would have asked myself questions such as these. And another thing – why my account? Am I entitled to take myself so seriously? And when I write, should it always be in terms of jazz in general? Or rather as a bass nerd? During this process I noticed that many memories which had nothing to do with jazz or my career resurfaced. Or are they related after all? Going through these personal tales again and reflecting on them was an interesting, often joyful and sometimes painful experience. I neither had to nor wanted to write an encyclopaedia. More than once I was alarmed by all the things that I found out about myself on the Internet. Allegedly I have cut records with musicians I can't even remember. I must confess that many such details are immaterial to me.

I love jazz. Not every kind. But there are areas that, in some cases, verge on obsessiveness. This is why I'm allowing myself to record my thoughts and my story emotionally at times, soberly at others, and, on occasion, furiously.

In good faith and to the best of my knowledge, but without any guarantees. Basically, these are the notes of a musically conscious man, ideally free of conceit. If there is such a thing…

1 A Stroke of Bad Luck

On Tuesday, 23 April 2007, around 7:30 p.m., I was sitting in a cab headed for the festively lit Berlin Philharmonic Hall. The driver didn't stop at the artists' entrance to drop me off as would have been the case normally – I was, after all, expected onstage just a few minutes later. Instead, he followed my instructions to take me to the emergency room of Berlin's Charité hospital. We drove past concertgoers waiting outside the Philharmonic Hall – they had no idea that I wouldn't be able to play that night. Nor could they imagine that at that very moment discussions were being held backstage as to whether the concert could take place at all or my colleagues of the Jan Garbarek Group would play without me. At that moment not even I realized that my twenty-five years of playing with the band had come to an end – and with it, my career as a jazz bassist.

In the afternoon, during a less than enjoyable sound check, I'd noticed the loss of my left hand's fine motor skills, which affected the confidence I had in my intonation. The reason behind my visit to the Charité hospital was the naïve question "What's going on?"

The year 2007 had been carefully planned by our management, Bremme & Hohensee. It was going to be a great tour year for the Jan Garbarek Group. About one hundred concerts were booked throughout Europe. On 22 April we'd played in Gronau, in Germany's far north. We'd decided to drive to Berlin – our next destination – right after the show, so that for once we'd be able to spend two nights in a row in the same hotel. Getting your laundry done occasionally and not having to pack and unpack your suitcase every day can be quite nice. One whole day not spent at the airport or on the autobahn! Our band was so punctual you could set your clock by us, so we were done at exactly 10:10 p.m. One set, as always without a break, and two encores. Our three technicians swiftly packed up our equipment. We got onto the autobahn to Berlin, and by two or three o'clock in the morning, we finally fell into our beds.

The next morning, that Tuesday, 23 April, I wanted to satisfy two long-standing culinary cravings: one for a Berlin bratwurst, the other for some Chinese food. I'm afraid this may sound contradictory and odd. I just wanted a change from the daily hotel breakfast buffets, which are the same everywhere.

We were staying at the brand-new Swissôtel on Augsburger Strasse. In its vicinity there was a Chinese restaurant with a whole bunch of bratwurst stands nearby. I stuck to my plan: first the bratwurst, then the Chinese.

But before that could happen a photographer asked me onto the hotel terrace for a photo-shoot. The pictures were supposed to feature alongside an article in the magazine *Jazzthetik*: my latest CD with ECM had just come out. *Stages of a Long Journey* was a live recording with the Stuttgart Radio Symphony Orchestra, Gary Burton, Jan Garbarek, Rainer Brüninghaus, Wolfgang Dauner, Marilyn Mazur, Reto Weber and Nino G.

After the shoot I set out to implement my culinary idea. As I left the hotel elevator, it felt like a piece of gum had got stuck to my left shoe. This was a posh, brand-new five-star hotel. Was there gum all over the place already? I looked at my sole, but there was nothing there! Strange. "So be it," I thought to myself.

More irritation outside the hotel: as I tried to step onto the sidewalk on the other side of the street, I tripped. Still, on to the bratwurst stand I went and consumed the sausage with great pleasure. After this amuse-bouche I strolled over to the Chinese restaurant, took a seat on the first floor, flipped through the pages of the menu and placed my order. Something indefinable was going on inside me. I'm incapable of describing what I felt, even today. It wasn't pain, I wasn't paralysed, I had no headache – basically I experienced no physical limitations of any kind. I can only describe it as the familiar feeling of "getting a cold."

Still, something wasn't quite right. I certainly enjoyed my food – to the extent that it's possible to enjoy German Chinese food. After paying the bill, I returned to the hotel – this time without the slightest hindrance. At this point it was half past two in the afternoon. I went up to my room and, as usual, got onto – not into – the bed: I wanted to avoid sleeping too deeply.

Everything seemed perfectly normal – except for this strange feeling which kept coming back. I briefly considered calling my wife. Maybe I should have. She might have suspected something right away: six months earlier I'd already experienced some sort of impairment at home in the South of France, where we'd been living for thirteen years in a small village near the beautiful little town of Uzès. To be on the safe side, I'd spent the night in hospital in Nîmes. But I'd blocked this out because it hadn't seemed important: nothing was detected and I was allowed to go home.

I now called our manager, Peter Hohensee, in his room and asked him to come. His mother had had a small stroke not long ago. As he stood in my room, he thought he noticed similar symptoms. He started asking me questions: Where were we? What time was it? What were we doing in Berlin?

Did he think I was stupid? He then asked me to do a few things, like walk along a line in the carpet. I did a decent job. Undoing and redoing my shoelaces was fine, too. Nonetheless, he suggested we call the emergency services.

Two paramedics, dressed in red, came from the fire department. They carried out the same tests, checked my blood pressure and blood sugar levels. In the end, they weren't able to find anything, adding, "We're no doctors, but we could drive you to a clinic." Meanwhile it was already half past four in the afternoon.

In the absence of any obvious negative findings, I decided to drive to the Philharmonic Hall for the sound check to see how my playing was affected. I put on my black stage suit so that I wouldn't have to return to the hotel after the rehearsal. Around five o'clock I got onstage. My colleagues had already heard that I'd had some sort of problem and were relieved to see me.

Sound checks were important to us for two reasons: first, to adjust the balance of our instruments in the hall; second, to prepare us for the sound we could expect onstage. For this purpose, we had two numbers that weren't necessarily part of the running programme, but perfectly suited for the task: one powerful and one mellow.

Our programme was relatively new. We had only performed it a few times. Right at the beginning, I had to play a very tricky melody. This demanded intense concentration. I now asked my colleagues to start playing this piece even though it wasn't normally part of our sound check.

I immediately noticed unusual intonation problems. I could still use my left hand normally: this hand was important for sound formation. The only problem was that my fine motor skills were missing – I no longer had a handle on the delicate details. I tried over and over again, without success. Jan said reassuringly: "Just leave out the melody. I'll play it today and you can do it again tomorrow."

Intuition or insight? In any case, I asked Peter Hohensee to drive me over to the Charité hospital. Just around the corner. Just to be safe. After leaving the stage, on our way to the car, all of a sudden there were more irritations: obvious problems with walking.

Then, however, came the demo effect: as soon as we arrived at the Charité's emergency room, all of my symptoms vanished. After the habitual wait, a youngish doctor appeared, and I described to him what had happened. During the examination there was a sudden power outage. Confusion all around: this sort of thing wasn't supposed to happen, not at this kind of hospital! Although the power was restored quickly, it wasn't long before we were plunged into darkness again – this time for much longer. Greater irritation.

Apparently, the examination didn't raise any obvious suspicions. Just the same, the doctor said, "It's probably better you stay here – for observation."

"But I have a concert tonight. I have to play!" I protested. My resistance was soon overcome. It was odd, though: I really was ready to stay and pack in the concert. Evidently, there was an inner voice telling me it wouldn't be all that bad to follow the doctor's advice.

Meanwhile, Peter Hohensee had driven back to the sound check, so I had to inform him by cell phone: "Just to be on the safe side, I've been asked to stay in hospital."

A long moment of shock. Then: "Let's see if your colleagues will play without you or if they prefer to cancel the concert."

I told the doctor that I really had to return to the hotel – that's where my luggage was. I added: "And we're leaving tomorrow morning. I have to pack." He was against it. "But I'm the only one who can do this. I have to go," I protested.

"Fine," he relented, "but I don't know anything about it."

I took this statement to mean that my symptoms couldn't be considered all that serious.

A taxi was booked for me, and I drove back to the hotel – without any sign of impairment. The first thing I did, was change clothes. My suit was meant for the stage. Wearing it in hospital made little sense – or much of an impression. Then I stuffed everything in my big suitcase and dragged the heavy thing back to the taxi stand.

The taxi drove past the brightly lit Philharmonic Hall and the concertgoers already waiting outside. Saddened, I was able to think only one thing: "Fuck!" What else?

Back at the Charité with my heavy accessory this time around, I listened to the sarcastic explanation of the young doctor on duty: "I have good news! We aren't doing any more MRI scans today." That's the examination in which you are pushed through a tube. He said it would be too dangerous because of the constant power outages. To my mind, if a doctor – from the "top" Charité hospital at that – said, "Then we'll just do it tomorrow," then clearly this meant I was OK. Without a doubt.

So there I was now, lying on a stretcher. From there I was able to observe curious things: a patient beside me evidently had got himself into trouble – he was being watched by two police officers. Another patient complained unremittingly that she had already been waiting for her diabetes medication for twelve hours. The nurses appearing every so often just rolled their eyes, barely trying to hide their impatience and annoyance. I was in no position to pass judgement on this strange scene.

Eventually, around the time the concert was supposed to have ended – assuming it had taken place at all – I was pushed into a dark room with several beds in it. All that sleeping, wheezing and snoring wasn't exactly uplifting. Still seeming perfectly fine, I was able to get ready for bed without assistance: bath, WC, pyjamas. Without any visible physical problems, I went to bed.

I can't remember anything after that. Did I black out or fall asleep normally? No idea.

The next morning, around six or half-past six, when the hospital got going again, a nurse appeared. As she went from one patient to the next, I noticed that I was no longer able to lift my left arm or leg. I could feel, I was pain-free, but I had lost all muscle power. I was irritated, but not especially concerned. Very naïvely, I thought: "The hospital will take care of it…"

The consultant on duty arrived relatively late – around nine, half past nine. He asked me to move the fingers of my left hand. They did move, albeit minimally, almost indiscernibly. "Oh, that's a good sign," he said.

I misinterpreted this statement, taking it to mean: "We'll take care of that straight away. Everything is going to be OK." Naïve as I still was, I asked: "And what's going to happen next? Are there any tablets for this?"

I can still remember his amused smile: "No, exercise is all that's left now. You'll have to go to a special rehab clinic."

No doubt it was clear to him then what my condition was. Unknowing, I gratefully took note of what he had said – the Jan Garbarek Group only had one more concert left to give before the upcoming break. The tour wasn't due to restart until summer or autumn – by then, I believed, I'd be in shape again thanks to the physiotherapy.

Later on, after I was discharged, I was able to see more clearly.

In the course of the morning, Peter Hohensee called me. My three colleagues had rallied to go ahead with the concert: Trilok Gurtu on drums, Rainer Brüninghaus on keyboards and Jan Garbarek on soprano and tenor saxophones. This requires courage and extraordinary concentration. Experience and a routine developed over decades allowed us to come up with emergency solutions barely fathomable to the audience. All it took was making the listeners forget the parts played by the missing colleague by replacing them somehow. My colleagues knew how to do that.

That morning the overdue examinations to establish the cause of my condition finally began. I was pushed into the tube. An occlusion, a dark spot, a blockage on the right side of the brain indicating a "right-hemispheric ischaemic cerebral infarct" was discerned – possibly triggered by high blood pressure that had gone undetected for years. Over the next three days I was pushed through the labyrinth of the Charité's corridors, from one examination to the next. During this time I made a remarkable discovery: every time a medical issue needs to be elucidated on German television, a doctor from the Charité hospital is a guest expert. The impression given is that this hospital really is the best, and nothing but the best care can be expected there.

Yet day-to-day operations were a disaster: there weren't enough staff. You would spend ages waiting on a stretcher in the hall. If it was draughty, it stayed draughty. On one occasion I lay unattended in a corridor for forty minutes, waiting helplessly for a staff member to come and get me.

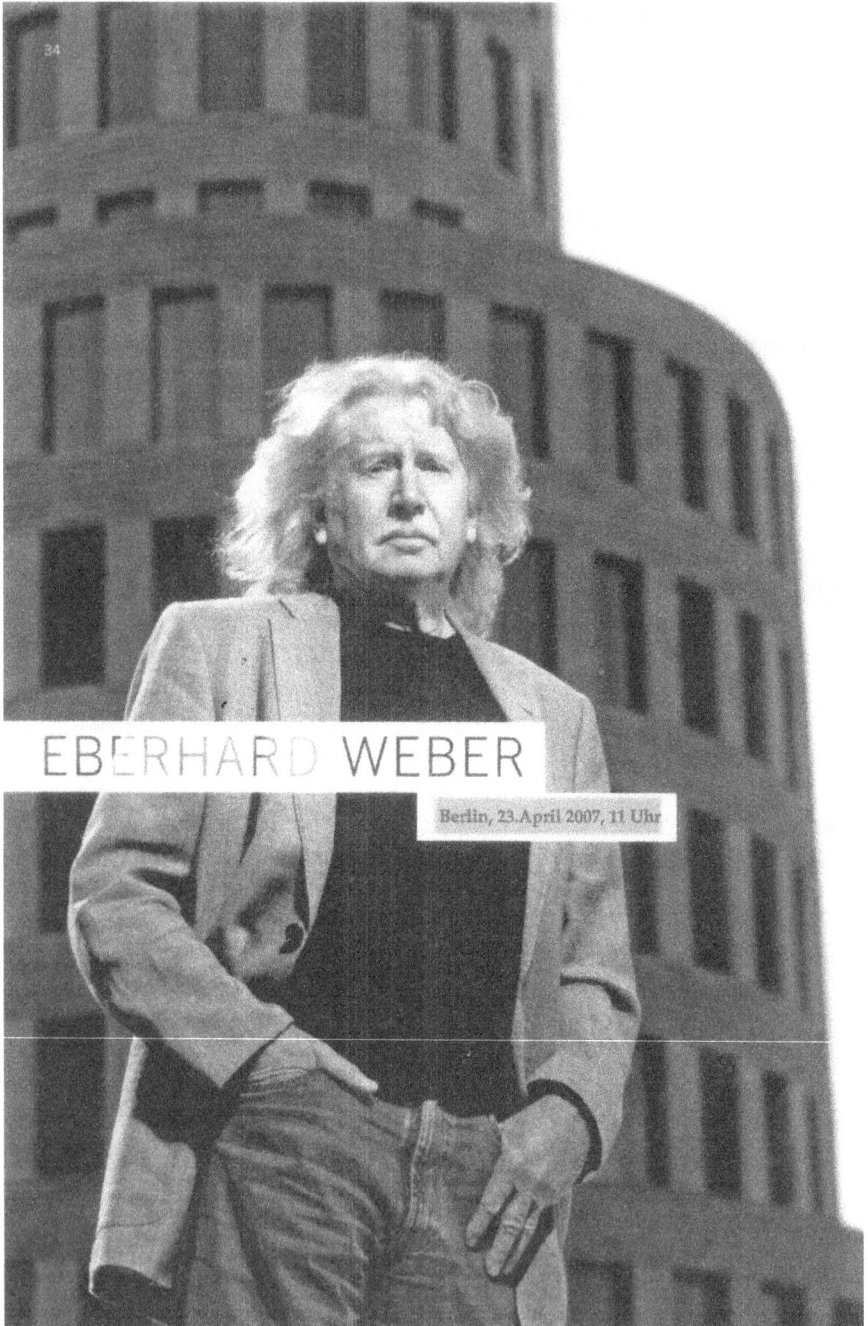

EBERHARD WEBER

Berlin, 23.April 2007, 11 Uhr

Figure 1: Press photo of Eberhard Weber taken about 30 minutes before his stroke. Berlin, 23 April 2007

In the field of neurology it is a well-known fact that rehab training has to begin as soon as possible after a stroke: it is mainly in the first three months that significant improvement can be made. Yet here, too, the Charité was full of surprises – in the week that I spent there, I spent only one hour with a therapist. Staff shortages.

A friend of mine from Berlin, Norbert Mauer, booked a freelance therapist I paid out of my own pocket to conduct crucial initial therapy with me on a daily basis. It was Norbert, too, who managed to secure a place for me in a rehab clinic so quickly – special clinics such as these are fully booked over long periods of time. After a week spent at the Charité, I was picked up by an ambulance and taken to the Median clinic in Grünheide, somewhere east of Berlin. My well-connected lawyer friend had been able to get me a place there even though the clinic was at full capacity. All things considered, I was given a nice room – a single room, at last!

It wasn't just the physical side of things that worried me. A lot still needed to be taken care of: my car stood in the underground car park of Marseille airport, where I'd left it and expected to return to soon. But the keys, vehicle documentation and car park ticket were all with me. Who takes care of stuff like that? Who has the time and means to? And what about clothing for a hospital stay? My suitcase was filled with almost nothing but stage wear.

Then the daily therapy sessions started. They involved various exercises and activities. I had to learn to use a wheelchair. I only had one side to steer with: my right leg and my right hand. My left side was completely blocked. Still uninformed – the therapists and doctors were very cautious – I continued to believe that I was going to be OK again soon.

The band's next concert took place in Lübeck, where my three colleagues performed without me again. The following day the newspaper read,

> Unfortunately Eberhard Weber did not appear as announced. Weber was unexpectedly hospitalized in Berlin last night, forcing the Jan Garbarek Group to perform without him. The bassist's absence was obviously noticeable as the low notes had to be taken over by the percussion, which failed to be a fully adequate replacement. Nevertheless, the three musicians managed to come together in a well-balanced performance that thrilled the audience. Standing ovations were given before the encores even started.

Apparently, things had gone surprisingly well. The concert was a success. It could be done without me… One might be tempted to get jealous.

On the other hand, I heard from our management that some of the concertgoers had returned their tickets and left after they found out that I wouldn't be performing. Was this something to be proud of?

The first part of the tour was now over. After the break things were supposed to "really" get going. In spite of the continued uncertainty surrounding my condition, I was convinced I would be joining the band then. It's hard to say if I was just naïve or if I was unwilling to recognize the severity of my situation. One thing is certain: I was sure that I would be back onstage again that autumn.

On 7 December 2007, the last concert of the tour took place. Without me. The press wrote: "In the wake of health issues affecting Eberhard Weber – one of the unmistakable sound components of the Garbarek Ensemble over the last three decades – the bass-player Yuri Daniel was brought onboard in the spring of 2007." I was out.

2 If Only I Knew

Let's begin with the most difficult question: what even is jazz? What Google and Wikipedia have put together tells us nothing about the music. They're dictionary definitions. Is it even possible to describe music? There certainly are mad, obsessed people who try to approach the unknown scientifically. In this vein, some journals have published studies on the topic of "love" – not the physical act, mind you. These studies register hormonal output and compile impressive analyses. Yet mysteries remain unsolved, and the inexplicable persists. Seeking refuge in poetry and using turns of phrase borrowed from wine tastings may be preferable. Or dipping into the syrupy sweetness of chansonniers, whose style can be just as florid. The vibraphonist Dave Pike – leader of the first professional formation I was a part of – once told a journalist in front of his colleagues in the Dave Pike Set, "Music is an island of beauty." When we heard this, we burst into laughter – Dave couldn't help but join in. It seems impossible to find definitive terms for emotions. The ECM slogan – "The most beautiful sound next to silence" – may not be particularly insightful, but there's something about it. At the very least, it makes for a good quote.

It's odd: I played jazz for over fifty years, but I'm incapable of describing what is so fascinating about this music, or why some people can relate to it, while others can't. Then there is the fact that opinions differ even when it comes to styles of jazz: Dixieland, swing, bebop, free, Latin, modern, cool. What variety! And what differences in opinion between these often irreconcilable factions!

If it's all jazz, why doesn't everybody love the same kind? I am no exception: there are types of jazz I've never liked and always found horribly boring, like Dixieland, for instance. In my youth New Orleans and Dixieland were seen as radically different when it came to old-time jazz. Why? New Orleans was played by Black people and Dixieland by White people. Easy enough to understand, but was it true? Musically at any rate, I could never tell the difference: it all sounded too basic. Back then, when I outed myself as a jazz musician, people would still ask me, "Old time or modern?" The question was both justified and annoying because I wanted to be taken seriously, and in this respect, old time just won't do: the few pitiful sounds that have to be plucked from the bass aren't worth the effort and, consequently, no fun at all. The fact that the double bass, coated in ugly black lacquer with white sides, was called "slap bass" says it all. At least mine was coated in clear lacquer.

The groovy black lacquer common back then suited the countless clownish ensembles – generally English bands – that appeared on TV in chequered suits intended to look comical. People must have thought it was hilarious when the bass player tugged on the trumpeter's braces – or when the trombone player's hat flew in the air with every crash of the cymbals. Good times guaranteed. At least the time hadn't come yet when thousands of spectators would fill entire stadiums and wet their pants every time someone ran across the stage, stopped without warning, and stared at the audience to signal that it was time to laugh.

I never had any contact with the old-time scene, so I haven't followed its potential development. I can imagine, though, that today Dixieland can only be heard in biergartens, at hotel brunches or on rafts on the river Isar in Munich – that is, if anyone is listening at all, and people's ears haven't been clogged by the gallons of beer flowing freely. Woody Allen's dabbling can't be considered a musical revelation, either. What is there to hear other than the same phrases repeated thousands of times?

Dixieland and free jazz are worlds apart, yet both call themselves jazz.

I will allow myself a strange definition: jazz is when the composer, the arranger or the performer makes it as hard as possible for the listener to follow the music – and everyone still enjoys it. This is what sets him apart from the alleged "new music." Jazz alone brings into play never-ending syncopation, countless harmonies and often uneven rhythms – or a combination thereof. Small correction: Brazilian music also makes liberal use of syncopation and harmonies. With jazz, on top of that, soloists are given to playing complicated stuff embedded in tricky harmonies – sometimes extremely fast, and at other times oddly slowly. As if they didn't want to be understood. It remains a mystery to me why incomprehensible music is met with such enthusiasm.

My definition also holds true for singing. Let's take opera: of course, Wagner scores call for outstanding technique, and no one can deny that coloratura requires skill. The exceptional vocal performances of many rock and pop singers are also obvious to fans – especially when they try to emulate their idols. Our vocal cords and the attached muscles are capable, if trained accordingly, of incredible expressiveness. Yet rock and opera fans – each at their own level of technical expertise – will easily be able to sing along to their favourite melodies, even if the quality of their singing isn't as good. Jazz alone demands what seems unnatural to many – harmonic shifts, changes in rhythm, complex melodic lines. This is the domain of experts – of Ella Fitzgerald or Bobby McFerrin and their colleagues – who are equipped with more than just the required craftsmanship. What's fantastic about jazz is its origin in improvisation, which makes it so one-of-a-kind. Jazz fans often love a song without remotely being able to sing its melody. This is not the case with classical music. My music teacher in grammar school, a Beethoven devotee, textualized the beginning of the master's famous Fifth Symphony. Who doesn't know the beginning of the first movement: bababa doooo … bababa daaaa. Then the swift, agitated continuation. I only remember a few lines of the "masterwork": *"Das Schicksal klooooopft … an deine Tüüüür."*[1] Followed shortly thereafter by: *"Was willst du, sprich, ich öffne dir, so komm zu mir...."*[2] You don't forget something like that. Unfortunately, I've forgotten the rest.

Some music appeals to me and some repels me. Why that is so is hard for me to explain – other than with the platitude that music, or art in general, is a private matter. Of the explanations provided by professionals, only the ones that remain free of emotions are of any use. Enraptured, some may welcome trance-like states. I prefer staying sober because trances automatically transfigure everything. Performing with a joint may be fun at first, but one of the reasons you imagine you are in seventh heaven is that you get over your mistakes faster: the quality of your playing is only ever perceived as being superior.

The biggest problem is the absence of criteria in jazz. Everyone can say what they want. While one says, "That was great," the other counters, "Spare me!" What now? Who decides? It's definitely an advantage that jazz is also synonymous with freedom, which is why in isolated cases, even inferior technique can be appreciated. The disadvantage – my disadvantage – is that waxing experience goes hand in hand with waning enthusiasm or naivety: you lose some of that carefree attitude. These days I immediately think I know which way the wind blows. Repetition bores me quickly. I run into big problems when hopeful young colleagues send me CDs with the request to give them my honest opinion. Most of the time I have to start by asking: "Why did you make the CD in the first place? Aren't there enough just like it already?"

Another unwelcome fact I've noticed is the many musical habits that have become established over the last decade and go completely unquestioned. Why does one bandmate, usually the drummer, always have to continue playing after the last chord? The conclusions used in classical music, effective and expeditious, have given way in jazz to a childish drive to play – or to vanity. One more "ping," another "pang," a "plash," a "bam": a typical feature of countless concerts and many studio recordings. Keith Jarrett and his trio effectively introduced abrupt endings – a praiseworthy exception tellingly appreciated by the audience, considering that apparently no jazz lover had ever thought of this solution before. This constant dragging on has become systemic. I admit that rock musicians are probably even more guilty of this. It's hard to find a

1. "Thus fate knoooocks … at your doooor."
2. "What do you want, speak, I'll open for you, so come to me."

rock concert in which individual songs don't end with endless drum or guitar solos. It would be interesting to carry out the Blindfold Tests: who can recognize the songs being played during these orgies? At least in the past this part of a concert served the purpose of publicly disposing of one's instruments.

Attentive listening will bring to light many things: Who starts a free introduction and when? Who dares to and with what kind of sound? As a rule, drummers are not so good at waiting – they like getting started immediately. To make up for it, they also prefer finishing late, ideally after everyone else. The "hashataplush" of the drums after a band's last chord is legendary. Maybe one more tender "pling" on the cymbals to finish – with the drumstick after a faster piece and the brush after a ballad. Additionally, as a rule, drummers fail to realize when the tempo "does a runner" or starts to drag. It's never their fault – that, at any rate, is how I've known it to be for over forty years.

It's similar with the choruses of the soloists: Is it really necessary to play a chorus six times? Wouldn't it be enough to play it three times or – better yet – just twice? It can certainly happen that performers run out of ideas – it all depends on the shape they're in. When this happens, it is customary to keep on playing in the hope that an idea will materialize. If it doesn't, which happens quite often, artificial dynamism helps – just keep beating the drum heads, the strings or the keys. If all goes well, it will be seen as temperament. That always goes down well! And isn't it natural – particularly for musicians – to try to be good showmen? I have colleagues who always have to stand in the first row. This is especially true when cameras are present, as for instance during televised recordings: Where is the red light shining? In which direction is the objective turning? Once this is established, it's all about nonchalantly shimmying into the scene in which one is most likely to appear on screen oneself. If not by oneself, then at the very least behind the soloist, miming enthusiasm while snapping one's fingers.

I am no exception in this department. On several occasions, I tried to redirect the attention of the cameramen from the hand on my fingerboard – which they always found quite exciting – to my face by slowly moving my plucking hand up and my head down. From the corner of my eye, I was able to spy that my hand and my face were reunited on the monitor. Voilà! And the cameramen got "awesome" shots, to use an expression beloved of TV professionals. Who knows them knows how to seduce them. During a tour of South America being filmed for a WDR (West German Broadcasting) documentary, I once started plucking some ropes strung across the canopy of a boat on the Amazon – I knew at once that this would make the cut. "Awesome! The bass player is plucking ropes on a boat on the Amazon." And? Did the scene appear in the documentary? Do I even need to confirm it?

Don't let my "plash-bam" derision fool you, though: I hold many drummers and percussionists in high regard. I was lucky enough to perform with many great musicians. Some even became friends, like Michael DiPasqua, whom I met at the Bottom Line jazz club in New York in the 1970s, when he performed with the vibraphone quartet Double Image. They were Ralph Towner's supporting act. I also got along with Mike on a non-musical level. To this day he puts up with long plane trips from Florida to visit me in southern Europe.

Figure 2: Michael DiPasqua and Eberhard Weber in front of Weber's house in southern France, 2008

The mystery that is jazz… Unlike classical music, jazz music doesn't make it easy to prove that a musician got something wrong. Yet it happens quite often! A critic may not have liked what he heard. But was it off? Compositions may be too complex, interpretations too personalized, performances too fast, too confusing. Onstage, however, the emergency brake has to be pulled quite often – if possible, in a manner that will leave the audience "unaware." The art of bringing back together a band falling apart has to be learned.

Since my stroke I've started listening to the radio again – consciously, on my computer or my TV. There still is no way I would let the radio tootle on incessantly in the background.

I've been living in France for more than twenty years now, near a World Heritage Site, the Pont du Gard, a multi-storeyed Roman aqueduct. In France there is a vast number of radio stations dedicated to jazz. I now get to benefit from this, giving as much thought as I want to what pleases me and what doesn't. It's incredible how many compositions today are still based on the familiar, partly overplayed twelve-bar blues. Yet I should briefly mention that the blues of the "cotton-picking era" has nothing to do with the twelve-bar form. In the "cotton-picking era," the kind of singing that developed within the Black population allowed for both fun and protest. To find out who came up with the still popular twelve-bar form, you would have to look somewhere else. At any rate, this twelve-bar form can be played for hours, if necessary, for weeks, and is ideally suited for the *Guinness Book of Records.* Jam sessions in particular can't do without it. Time and time again, people are astounded that musicians who have never met before – an American pianist, a Belgian trumpeter, a Russian trombonist, a Japanese guitarist, a German bass player and an Australian drummer, for example – can just start playing the blues in Bb together without ever having practised as a group. The well-versed, on the other hand, will know at once what point a performance has reached. It then becomes possible to join in at any time. On top of that, it sounds perfect, practically flawless, and provided that you stick to a few parameters, such as harmonies, the possibilities for improvisation are boundless. There is, of course, a lot of repetition. Yet in all probability, no two blues solos are the same – even though there are millions.

I don't want to give the wrong impression: I, too, love this form of blues and have contributed considerably to its propagation over my fifty years on the stages of the world. But at the same time, I wanted to explore new horizons. Young musicians today are no different: many get off the beaten track, try out new concepts and develop tricky new structures.

Hard as it may be to explain what jazz is, the answer to another question is just as challenging: Why does one become a musician, a jazz musician at that? Is it because of talent, joy or a special connection? Pleasure? A dream? Probably, as so often, a combination of various elements. Once you reach a certain age, the questions start. At this point your reasoning has to withstand scrutiny. What are the advantages of playing jazz? Is it all that different from the repertoire of classical music? After all, no two classical concerts are purported to be the same even though the notes are always identical. In jazz, on the other hand, we can invoke individuality and relative freedom through improvisation.

It's wonderful that, as far as jazz is concerned, musicians with varying degrees of technical skill can be as convincing as the greatest stars and go further with less. Rather than an exercise in perfection, jazz is a constant creative process. Of all the reasonably well-respected bass players, I dare call myself the least technically accomplished. I was perfect – at hiding my hang-ups. Even my trademark electric double bass, this strange incorporeal construct, wasn't perfect. No one noticed. Yet night after night I had to take into consideration shortcomings in the tonal range, avoiding certain regions, excluding higher registers or specific strings – or, alternatively, consciously making use of special regions in order to introduce them as stunning effects, routinely making all of these inadequacies inaudible. In spite of this, or precisely because of it, I managed to be seen as unique, exceptional even.

As far as I know, when I started playing this unusual bass, there was nothing comparable on the market. My device took a long time to be painstakingly brought up to scratch – by me, by guitar and bass makers, by pickup producers. How could it be any different when no experience was available? Much, much later, the market filled up with instruments of a newer kind. Understandably, such developments are time-consuming and expensive. And they require the conviction that enough people will be interested in "taking the road less travelled." In contrast, the market for electric guitars in the rock and pop industries was booming. That's where the real money was. But where does that leave the simple luthier?

There is no such thing as a perfect instrument: not because of any production issues, but because of the player's never-ending moaning. I have never met one who was entirely satisfied with his instrument.

I don't know what Stradivarius-owning millionaires have to say to that. Is there an even better "Strad" to lust after? Or is it better to switch to a Guarneri?

On a brighter note, in our line of business, acquisitions can be made for "just a few thousand euros." Still a lot of money, but at least we don't have to deal with astronomical fees or pander to sponsors. I may be wrong, but I have yet to meet a bass player with a Stradivarius.

When it comes to my intonation, it was pretty much perfect. In spite of my inadequate, twisted finger technique, I managed to produce tones that were impeccably clean. To put things into context, the great classical composer Richard Strauss is rumoured to have said, "A pure tone on a contrabass is pure luck!" The man has my greatest sympathy.

Many years ago I had the chance to meet one of my bass heroes, Red Mitchell. The American bassist had acquired an entirely unorthodox technique: pentatonic tuning. It must be said that the double bass is usually tuned in fourths. Fifths are technically not practicable because the span of the left hand simply isn't big enough. However, for the significantly smaller violoncello, fifths are ideal. Oddly enough, the American bass player Oscar Pettiford was also celebrated as a cellist. Only a few people knew that he tuned his cello in fourths, just like his bass. No wonder he was able to move seamlessly from one instrument to the other. Besides, to all intents and purposes, he didn't "play" the cello: he merely "plucked" it. And that doesn't count! He was merely hyped up by the jazz radio presenters of the time – as is so often the case, against their better judgement.

Getting back to Red Mitchell, it was interesting for me to witness what brilliant results he could achieve with his exotic finger technique. Red was an extremely pleasant bloke. Unfortunately, my knowledge of English was less than basic when I met him back then. That's why, when we spoke, I didn't really understand how he managed to physically overcome this oddity. That's only half the truth, though: I felt immensely honoured that this great American bass player would have anything to do with me. I was "on the upswing" at the time, celebrated as fresh talent. I'm sure that Red Mitchell, who was then living in Europe, realized he was dealing with a young German musician who had already acquired some merit. He therefore thought he was among his own kind and would be able to talk shop with me. This pride led me to listen to him in a pointedly casual manner even though I understood nothing of what he was saying.

Unfortunately, I was much too shy to ask for clarification. If anything, being "of equal rank," I kept nodding to convince him I was "in on it." I don't even know how he tuned his bass. Should it have been the likely violoncello tuning, he would have had to lower the low E string two more notes to C. The A string would have just had to be brought down a bit to G, D would have stayed the same, and G tuned to A, which produces a somewhat more brilliant sound. I'm sure all of this was explained to me in great detail – but it was all Greek to me. Thus it remains a mystery, and I, utterly useless as a witness. It's only now that I can really see this. It's a pity, really.

Mitchell impressed me because initially he would play in a wholly unspectacular way, just like everybody else. Suddenly, though, he would insert fascinating little embellishments that baffled me: "How does he do that?" This meant his technique was phenomenal, but it only shone through occasionally. He didn't seem to need to dazzle throughout, playing unassumingly instead. What remains is his unique sound. Regardless of how he produced it.

So, for the first time in sixty years, I now ask myself: what is jazz, actually? Representatives of the ultimate truth, like the pope of jazz, Joachim-Ernst Berendt, have had less and less trouble with this question over the years. But I'll get to that later. I admit that in the time I was active, I didn't grapple with the issue, simply because I was more concerned with myself. Always on tour or in the studio, I was hardly interested in other bands or musicians. It's only at festivals that we would meet.

Also, I was never an "explorer." I was always of the opinion that anyone with anything worth saying would find a way to say it. Real talent doesn't go unnoticed. To this day, I find it hard to give young people advice.

These days there are conservatoires all over the place – something we certainly would have wished for in the past. On the other hand, while young musicians today are perfectly trained and play at a level of technical skill that we "old folks" can't keep up with, everything sounds the same. It may well be that young musicians today are forced into a sort of hectic industriousness because the market has changed so much: I am very glad that I don't have to start out now. Perhaps this is precisely what helped my musical evolution: when I decided to become a professional, I had had years to slowly find my own way. I wanted to wait until I was sure the time had come. But perhaps I should start telling my story from the very beginning.

3 Under the Grand Piano

I know relatively little about my parents. Unfortunately, I didn't get around to finding out more about them in their lifetime. Yet I lived with them for a long time – much too long.

We never really talked. Speechlessness reigned in our home, where adhering to bourgeois conventions was prioritized. To the outside world, we projected the image of a harmonious family. In reality, my mother was very dominant, and my father often went his own way. As a child, and later as an adolescent, I rarely thought of asking my parents any questions, of taking any interest in their story. Now it's too late, considering that I am the last descendent of my family.

As the son of a musician, my musical career was more or less predestined. My father, Hans Weber, was a professional cellist. Born and raised in Berlin-Wilmersdorf, he studied musicology and obtained a PhD there. He was taught by Hugo Becker, who was a famous cello teacher back then. It was a very different time with a very different idea of sound. My father told me that his teacher once suggested: "I would insert a little vibrato here!" Since the vibrato had already gained widespread acceptance by then, all my father could do was grin roguishly.

In the early years, he worked his way up to the position of orchestral musician, supplementing his salary by playing at the weekends for one of the many dance ensembles of Bernard Etté, the locally renowned leader of café orchestras. He had put together various ensembles that regularly played music for people to dance to at various locations. Etté drove from one to the other to do the honours and perform a few party pieces on the violin – a kind of André Rieux of the 1920s and '30s. The respective musicians were recruited from the surrounding orchestras. My father played the cello, of course, but evidently, he also played the banjo. I was never able to find out what he played on it, though – my questions remained unanswered. I suppose it must have been enough to just "scrub" a little rhythm without paying too much attention to accurate chords. These "dance gigs" were popular with musicians: they represented a welcome addition to orchestra wages. His best friend, a fellow musician, was in charge of the weekly allocation of jobs with Bernard Etté. When my father asked his friend why he was getting so few gigs, his friend replied: "Where business begins, friendship ends."

According to my father, the allocation of gigs had to be paid for with a "donation," a percentage of the proceeds, which he did not agree with.

I can't say much about what happened before I was born. My parents' wedding, their professional life – this all took place more than eighty years ago. Who told what story? Who claimed it? Was it embellished? Is it even true? Eighty years! Wikipedia and Google haven't looked into my parents' story yet. Other witnesses died long ago. I have to fall back on a few cues, and even they are seventy years old. One memory is of my father being engaged by the Stuttgart Philharmonic in the 1920s. It was the year of Beethoven's anniversary. When it was over, he couldn't hear the "Fifth" anymore, the one that starts with "bababa doooo." That was long before I was born. Later, Dr Hans Weber hired himself out as a private music teacher, giving cello and piano lessons.

My father did not have a strong Berlin dialect. Instead, he toiled away at acquiring a slight Swabian accent: as the choirmaster of a men's chorus in Tübingen, he wanted to blend in with its proud denizens.

But he did have what Berliners used to call a "ready joke." I remember that for a while some Jehovah's Witnesses paid us a visit almost every Sunday morning. At some point, my father decided, "We're not going to let them in anymore."

This is exactly what happened until once again they showed up outside our flat – a neighbour had left the door to our building open. "Don't open it," my father whispered while they knocked on our door. But they didn't give up – until my father finally shouted through the closed door, "What do you want?"

Their answer echoed through the hallway: "We bear glad tidings!"

To which my father replied: "Just leave them there. I'll pick them up later!"

During the war my father was conscripted as a so-called "constable."[1] Whenever there was an alert, even in the middle of the night, he would take off in his police uniform, which left me deeply impressed. The actual perils of war made no impression on me whatsoever. At least that's how I remember it – my sister and I were too little, we couldn't understand why the adults would become so frantic at the wailing of sirens. Did we even know what danger was? But I was very impressed by my father's stories – we called him Pipin – or else I would have forgotten them. He told us, for instance, about the time Adolf Hitler drove past our local station in his special train. The entire stretch had to be secured half a day earlier. Pipin watched as the so-called Führer's train – with its saloon coach in the middle – passed our town, flanked by lorries with

---

1. "*Schutzmann*".

monstrous anti-aircraft guns and auxiliaries, on its way to Berchtesgaden, to Obersalzberg, where the "Führer" would spend his summer holiday. Or was it on its way back to Berlin? My father never told me what he felt when he stood there, watching the train go by. He wasn't a Nazi, though – that much seems certain to me. I don't know of a single incident that would lead me to believe that my parents sympathized with the Nazis in any way.

Esslingen am Neckar wasn't destroyed during the war. It remained a beautiful little medieval town with a great number of timber-frame houses. At least it did, until after the war, when the town councillors, filled with envy at seeing so many towns rebuilt, started tearing down houses to replace them with the architectural monstrosities of the post-war years. In Esslingen, as in so many places, stupidity caused more damage to the townscape than the war (although both must be closely connected).

I'm pretty sure that only one bomb was dropped on my hometown. One night, it destroyed a small section of the train station, a mere kilometre away from our flat. Prior to that, there had once again been an air-raid warning and my father, answering the call of duty, would have been long gone. My mother chased us children out of bed, we'd already reached the staircase, and just as we were about to start running downstairs to the air-raid shelter, the three of us were hurled to the floor by the massive blast. I remember seeing the windows in front of me in the staircase, and wondering why none of the panes of glass had shattered.

Born in Stuttgart, my Swabian mother was employed there as a secretary or an accountant for Allianz when she met my father. When and on what occasion this was, remains unclear – as does the question of when my parents moved to Esslingen, a small town on the river Neckar, fourteen kilometres away from Stuttgart. From this union, my sister Gisela was born in 1936. Acting on the obvious wish to produce a son and heir, my parents brought me into the world in 1940, unasked, and in the middle of the war at that. Most likely I was conceived in Esslingen though I was then born in Stuttgart. As I was born in a district called Stuttgart-Hedelfingen, I am bureaucratically blessed with being a Stuttgarter – and having to write "Stuttgart-Hedelfingen" every time I am asked for my place of birth. A popular accumulation of letters and hyphens for which there hardly ever is enough space on the forms I have to fill out.

I grew up in a flat on the raised ground floor of a beautiful old brick villa with stucco ceilings at 12 Schelztorstrasse. The elderly owner of the building, Frau Pfleiderer, lived above us. My mother had a reasonable singing voice and was of the opinion that it was good enough to interpret Hugo Wolf and Franz Schubert lieder. Inevitably, at every family gathering, the request "Hilde, sing something" would be made.

Figure 3: Eberhard Weber as a four-year-old

For decades on end, her vehement protests would be quelled after three requests at most. I was embarrassed by this ritual as much as by the fact that, in order to create the unavoidable classical vibrato, she would wobble her chin. I wasn't sure how other singers managed to sing without wobbling their chins. I can't recall if her chin movements really brought about anything resembling a vibrato. At any rate, her performances were regularly followed by amicable applause.

My father accompanied my mother on the piano, which he didn't play nearly as well as the cello. This didn't bother anyone, though, and inevitably encores would follow, prolonging my misery. It didn't cross anybody's mind that my father would have been able to play a far better solo cello suite by J. S. Bach. Even then, vocals triumphed over instrumentals in the Weberian inner circle. At church, I always felt uncomfortable when my father's voice – croaky but loud – joined in with the parish choir, which was notorious for lagging behind the organ. As a musician, he sang accurately, logically following the organ – even though no one else did. Carefully, the parishioners would turn around to see whose singing was "off." My greatest fear was that they would see me sitting next to him – turning very red.

In the intimacy of our home, I wasn't prepared to play classical party pieces on the cello. I can't remember ever having played a children's song or a Christmas carol for my family – I always refused. It wasn't until much later, after I'd defected to the bass, that I felt the urge to perform at our Weberian family get-togethers, if only to provoke the conservatives and show them which way the wind was now blowing. When relatives paid us a visit, my jazz friends Martin Schwäble and Roland Wittich would just "happen to be there." Their instruments, too, would just "happen to be" in their car or on their Vespa – just outside our building!

Once in a while, my father would be asked to help out with concerts held in the town church, especially if important performances including solo parts for the cello were scheduled. Occasions like these called for a professional. My mother, a long-time member of the church choir, put her venerated general music director, Hans-Arnold Metzger, in touch with my father, so that the church orchestra, which consisted only of amateurs, would be better equipped for Bach's oratorios and cantatas. The members of my father's string quartet were also put to good use on such occasions.

Gisela, my sister, was a good pianist. We got on, which was just as well because we had to share a room. In the evenings and at night, from behind drawn curtains, we became experts at identifying different brands of cars by the sound of their engine. I'm not at all sure if it's still possible today to tell a BMW apart from a VW Passat by its sound alone. Back then, it was easy. Mercedes, Ford, Opel, Volkswagen and DKW: these are the makes I still remember. Oh, and the one-of-a-kind Tempo, a three-wheeled lorry that would regularly tip over when it reached a bend near our building, right in front of a stationery store called Simon. The hasty reloading of spilt merchandise would complete the thrilling spectacle.

There weren't as many car brands then as there are now, and every car had its own sound – identifying a Beetle from afar was no great feat. Yet, for us children, these nightly games became an early form of auditory training, which – although we weren't aware of it at the time – taught us to listen and discriminate. While I don't have perfect pitch, like many active musicians, I let the sound of my instrument guide me. People with perfect pitch can instantly identify a musical note, which can go so far as to make transposing quite painful. While I am not one of these people, it only takes me a short moment of concentration to think about where on my bass a given note is located until I can name it. Later on, I knew exactly what the open strings on my bass sounded like, and when I played along to a piece in my head, I could recognize the key in which the composition was written. During jam sessions, I was able to join in quickly, which was also due to the fact that, very early on, I'd started playing dance music with my friend, the pianist Martin Schwäble. Martin played quite nicely, but in a somewhat unsophisticated, happy-go-lucky kind of way, which meant that on occasion, part of a piece would be off. Playing with him taught me to react quickly, almost instantly. I am still grateful to my unwitting teacher. It was thanks to him that years later, while playing with my long-term musical partner, Rainer Brüninghaus, I was able to rely on my rapid reaction time. Rainer loves to break free, to change things up, to wreak havoc – even with structures he has arranged himself. He is a pianistic free spirit – safe in the knowledge that the band is able to follow him. I always enjoyed having him chase me through the whole circle of fifths, not knowing where we were headed or what came next – I was almost always able to get in on the fun. It was hugely enjoyable every time one of these spontaneous tours de force succeeded. Rainer knew that he could get away with it with me. It was wonderful that we could have such a good time onstage – a welcome distraction, a little secret the audience knew nothing of.

Even as a young jazz fan, it didn't take me long to realize that onstage there is a life of its own that the audience is seldom aware of. During one of the Johnny Dankworth Big Band's concerts in the Liederhalle in Stuttgart, for instance, I noticed the grins on the astonished band-members' faces right after their drummer played some crazy stuff. By that stage, I had already gained enough musical experience to laugh with them. During an extended "fill" in 4/4 time, the drummer had suddenly started playing a "trick fill," in which your only chance not to miss the next cue is to count along without missing a beat. I'm sure the audience enjoyed this, too: the musicians onstage made it obvious that something funny must have happened. As to what exactly this was, though, the listeners had no idea. I won't hide that it can be fun when you realize that the audience is clueless. Younger drummers, usually from the jazz-rock scene, often take pleasure in briefly "disrupting" a groove with a rhythm from the realm of triplets. You then have to keep a rhythm in 4/4 time with these triplets until eventually the triplets fall back into 4/4 time – which requires concentrated precision. Although this gives a song a striking musical effect, it also threatens to trip up the other musicians. This "trick" rhythm can only be attempted with experienced and, ideally, prepared colleagues – it is a gimmick of specialists on tour to shake things up a bit!

But I'm jumping ahead: back to Esslingen. The consequences of the war were getting more tangible, and it became harder for my sister and me to continue playing our nightly guessing game: fewer and fewer cars were driving past our home. Petrol was in very short supply – to the point that cars with wood carburettors were introduced. Almost nobody remembers this today. A boiler mounted in the rear powered these cars with steam. Every so often the drivers would have to get out of their cars to stoke the fire. Only the privileged were able to secure this post-war mode of locomotion for themselves. Dressed in a suit, white shirt and tie, they would add coal or wood to the fire, like firemen on a steam locomotive.

My sister once had the opportunity to play a piano concerto by Haydn with the school orchestra in the parish hall of Esslingen, the most exciting concert hall of my childhood. I was extremely impressed – as were my parents, of course. It remained Gisela's only concert. She was never interested in pursuing a musical career – something I could never understand. I had been dreaming of it for as long as I could remember. I felt the thrill of the stage regardless of whether I was on it as a cellist or a page turner. After passing the *Abitur* exam, Gisela started working at SDR (South German Broadcasting), in the sound archive, which she was eventually in charge of. At SDR she met Carl-Johann Schäuble, who was then an editor in the news department. The result: Gisela Weber turned into Gisela Schäuble. In her spare time, she wrote a very interesting book. Radio and television editors regularly came to her, asking for music to go with particular scenes, films or programmes. She decided to classify their inquiries, and put together a register of "musical moods" – cheerful, sad, romantic, stormy, angry, menacing, tender. In short: everything that people in radio and television thought their work required emotionally. Gisela had a strong affinity for music and an encyclopaedic knowledge of the classical repertoire to boot. When she showed me the thick, purpose-bound tome, I was sorry that this highly informative book wasn't commercially available.

As mentioned earlier, I started dreaming of a career onstage at a young age. I had set my sights on the parish hall in Esslingen – my personal Carnegie Hall. At least, as a page-turner for the pianists performing with my father, my wish was partly granted. Indispensable for pianists reading sheet music during a performance, page-turning requires experience: one has to know – or rather, feel – how many bars the pianist "stores" in his head so as not to turn the page too soon or too late. This is how I became acquainted with the entire canon of string quartets, and many piano quintets, too, by Dvořák, Schubert, Schumann and Brahms. I can't remember anything ever going wrong. Not on my account, at any rate. Decades later, I once witnessed an orchestra falling apart – the Ansbach Bach Orchestra. Pierre Boulez was conducting Bach's *The Art of Fugue*. Suddenly, chaos broke out. Awkward silence followed. Then: "One more time, please, from bar…." The performance continued – with much higher levels of concentration this time around. It isn't all that unusual for an orchestra to fall out of sync onstage. When it is brought back together skilfully, though, nobody is any the wiser. I, too, had to fake it sometimes, even during solo concerts, pretending that the odd shift in harmony or rhythm was a stroke of genius – deliberate, of course. At such moments, routine is a big help.

Let me take this opportunity to mention one of the peculiarities of my musical taste. Be it the chorale of Bach's 'St John Passion' or 'St Matthew

Passion', or any other hymn for that matter, I could never understand why so many conductors insert a second of reaction time after every other line of sung text. If you count along, you'll notice that it's actually pure 4/4 time. But every time an additional crotchet gets added on after the last rhyme, it turns into 5/4 time.

Here is one example (only for readers who are up for it) from a Paul Gerhardt hymn:

> *Oh Haupt voll Blut und Wunden,*
> *Voll Schmerz und voller Hohn,*
> *Oh Haupt, zum Spott gebunden*
> *Mit einer Dornenkron;*
> *Oh Haupt, sonst schön gezieret*
> *Mit höchster Ehr' und Zier,*
> *Jetzt aber höchst schimpfieret:*
> *Gegrüßet sei'st du mir!*[2]

It should be sung as follows:

> *Oh* (that's the upbeat)
> *Haupt voll Blut und Wuhunden,*
> *Voll Schmerz und voller Hohn,* (two, three)
> *Oh Haupt, zum Spott gebuhunden*
> *Mit einer Dornenkron;* (two, three)
> *Oh Haupt, sonst schön geziehiret*
> *Mit höchster Ehr' und Zier,* (two, three)
> *Jetzt aber höchst schimpfiehiret:*
> *Gegrüßet sei'st du mir!* (two, three, four)

Yet this is how the majority do it:

> *Oh* (that's still the upbeat)
> *Haupt voll Blut und Wuhunden,*
> *Voll Schmerz und voller Hohn,* (two, three, four, five!!)
> *Oh Haupt, zum Spott gebuhunden*
> *Mit einer Dornenkron;* (two, three, four, five!!)
> *Oh Haupt, sonst schön geziehiret*
> *Mit höchster Ehr' und Zier,* (two, three, four, five!!)

---

2. "O sacred head surrounded / by crown of piercing thorn; / O royal head so wounded, / reviled and put to scorn: / death's shadows rise before you, / the glow of life decays, / yet angel hosts adore you / and tremble as they gaze!" W. H. Monk, *Hymns Ancient and Modern*, translated by H. W. Baker and J. W. Alexander (London: J. Alfred Novello, 1861).

And so on... Totally illogical! Some overeager conductors even conduct in six-four time. What is more, the "O" turns into a heavy upbeat that pulls the whole thing down. How on earth is one to reach heaven this way? Interpretations of this kind remove all lightness – making way for a sad mood instead. Every time I hear this, I find it abstruse. Of course, I could find out if the composer placed fermatas above the last notes, but not even that would convince me of the soundness of this idea.

Have you ever noticed that the same forced fermatas have been adopted for national anthems?

Music loomed large in our home. All the radio ever played was classical music. After the war my father had set his sights on a French station, scanning the airwaves for shortwave broadcasts of orchestral concerts in Paris every Sunday morning. Often it was the big stars of the time who played – cellists my father mentioned all the time. He knew one or two of them from his time as a student. Undeterred by medium-wave interference and fading, we listened to all the cello concerts, over and over again. Sometimes Pierre Fournier was the soloist, at other times it was the Italian Enrico Mainardi. Less frequently, it would be Pablo Casals or Gaspar Cassadó. This was the crème de la crème of the time. There really wasn't anybody much better than that. Today there are dozens of brilliant soloists for every instrument imaginable, all ploughing through the market, striving to secure decent gigs.

Shortly after the war my father suddenly became very popular as a piano teacher. There were several American GIs who wanted lessons from him so that they could play the *Warsaw Concerto*, which sounded like Rachmaninov, but was, in fact, written by a British film composer, a certain Richard Addinsell, for the movie *Dangerous Moonlight* in 1941. Radio stations played it all the time back then. Not one of the GIs had ever touched a piano – they soon realized that learning to play a musical instrument is a lengthy process. One after the other, they stopped showing up.

Our town, Esslingen, was in the American occupation zone. I still remember the grownups talking about this over the last days of the war: Who would occupy our town? Would it be "the Frenchman" or "the *Ami*"?[3] There were rumours that the two armies were approaching from different directions. Everybody hoped that the *Ami* would be the first to conquer us. He was. "The Frenchman" only made it as far as Tübingen, forty-two kilometres away from my hometown.

"The *Ami*" was welcome in Esslingen. I, too, had a few experiences that made me like him. Not far from our flat, my future secondary school, the Georgii Gymnasium, was being used by the Americans as a barracks. When my friends and I saw the uniformed soldiers in the street, we got into the habit of following them: there was a good chance they'd drop a few squares of chocolate. I don't know if the soldiers did this on purpose or not. Avidly,

3. "The Yank".

we would scoop up the pieces and let them melt in our mouths, as slowly as possible. Chocolate of this quality wasn't available in Germany. All we had here was something called "Lukullus," a product made to resemble chocolate – Germany's first post-war candy. The two kinds were worlds apart, so we never missed a chance to follow the GIs.

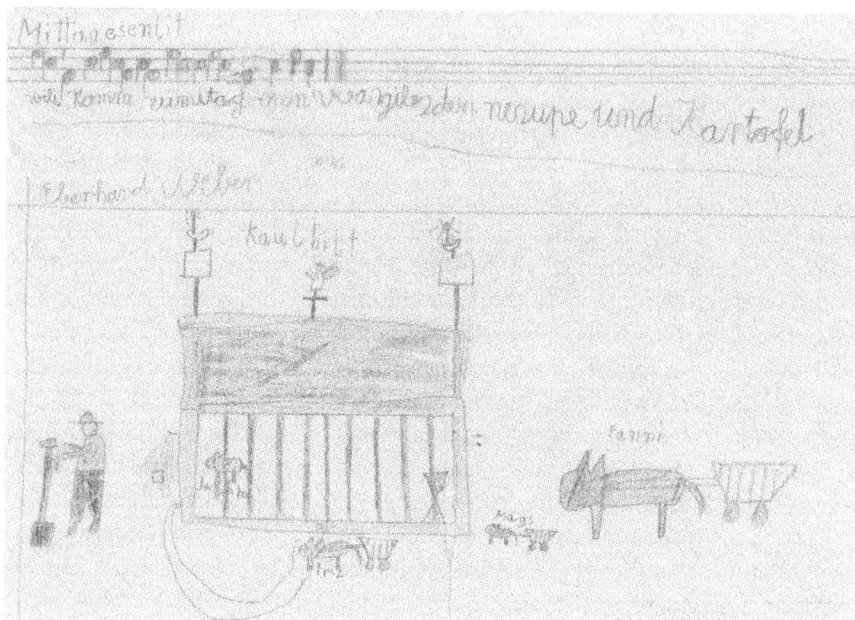

Figure 4: Eberhard Weber's first "composition," 1947

There were "mean Americans," too. Big lorries full of German prisoners of war jammed together in the back would drive past our building. It was the middle of summer, and the heat must have been unbearable for the captured German soldiers. Everyone in the neighbourhood would fill any available containers with drinkable liquids and throw them onto the towering transport vehicles, hoping they wouldn't break. To the great frustration of all involved, this is exactly what happened most of the time. Over and over again, heaps of glass shards had to be swept up. This all happened in front of our building because the bend in the road forced the lorries to slow down as they prepared to make the turn. On the back of each lorry there was an American soldier, armed with a rifle. Some drivers slowed down even more to facilitate the distribution of beverages. But sometimes – less frequently –angry armed escorts would shoot in the air to intimidate the helpers and speed things up. Among the German prisoners, some were seeing their own homes from the trucks for the first time since the end of the war. This is precisely what happened to our baker, Herr Nürk, nicknamed "Dr Bakernirk," just a few houses down the street from us. Having returned from the battlefield unscathed, he was now on his way to a POW camp, unable to stop and greet his family. To me this all seemed alien and exotic. My five-year-old self gazed at these proceedings in amazement – like I had before, when the night sky turned blood-red, when Stuttgart was burning.

Another German soldier who had returned from the war was my paternal cousin, Klaus Schochow. Klaus was being held by the Americans in our immediate vicinity, near Ludwigsburg. Oddly enough, he enjoyed remarkable freedom as a POW, showing up at our home every now and again. More importantly, though, he managed to smuggle food out of the camp, which, it was rumoured, was punishable by death. I recall a large metal container full of dried potatoes, which my mother, a rather unskilled cook, prepared for us every day. At a later point he somehow managed to get hold of a whole cart full of pumpkins for us. It took years before I was able to enjoy the taste of this fruity vegetable again.

After his release, Klaus asked if we would put him up temporarily. The question now was: how was he to make a living without having received any formal training? I was much too young to understand these discussions. At any rate, Klaus decided to learn to play the transverse flute. From that point on he practised tirelessly in the only room in the building in which he wouldn't bother anyone: our laundry room, in the cellar. Sure enough, after a successful audition, he quickly secured his first job with the Stuttgart Philharmonic. Not much later, he even managed to get accepted by the orchestra of the Hamburg State Opera. And, sometime in the summer, he was summoned to "Olympus" itself: the Bayreuth Festival. As I later found out from him, since the audience could not see into the pit, the orchestra there was permitted to perform in street clothes or, in true Bavarian fashion, in lederhosen.

I never discussed with my "Wagner-certified" cousin how it can be that even I, a schooled musician, can't clearly hear what Wagner instructed his singers to do. My contention is that, owing to the Wagnerian "extreme vibrato," it is impossible to determine not only where exactly in a bar the notes should be located, but also what the notes in question should be. A Wagner vibrato is quite capable of vacillating between two to three notes. Singers of Wagner's operas never sing without a vibrato, unless they are dealing with the most extreme of pianissimos, which are whispered theatrically. The mere task of analysing a vocal quartet verges on the impossible: four people all vibrating at once, one more fiercely than the next. If you don't have the partitions in front of you, there is no way to tell where exactly the cues and the notes belong.

After the war, as far as I was concerned, the greatest highlights of all were the musical evenings at our home – they took place far too seldom. On these occasions my father would invite colleagues from SDR Stuttgart's symphony orchestra, three of whom he had started a string quartet with. Herr Kessler played the first violin – he held the same position in the orchestra. He brought along the second violinist, Herr Schumann, and the viola player, Herr

Rottweiler. The latter was subsequently furloughed without notice by Sergiu Celibidache, the new, competent chief conductor – dismissals were not possible back then. Herr Rottweiler – *nomen est omen*[4] – was committed to the breeding of dogs and had chosen to regularly leave his viola in his locker after rehearsing with the orchestra. Needless to say, the quality of his sound soon failed to meet the standards of Maestro Celibidache's keen ear. Now Herr Rottweiler had even more time for his beloved dogs – and for the string quartet. He always seemed to have been prepared for these performances – I can't recall anything that would suggest otherwise. Some evenings there would be a pianist, too, magically turning the string quartet into a piano quintet.

These quartets and quintets took place about once a month – not often enough. But I can proudly report that this is how I came to hear almost everything written for quartets and quintets at such a young age, turning into a kind of mini expert. These were wonderful experiences – defining moments for my future. When the musicians had finally gathered in the music room and finished warming up, the most thrilling sounds would fill our home for two hours. By ten o'clock it was all over: much too soon! It could have gone on all night if you'd asked me. I loved these rehearsals; the musician in me was already stirring. I was allowed to stay in the room: lying under the grand piano was permitted as long as the pianist was present. This is where I learned to love the unbelievably potent sound of a piano from below. Later on, in the course of my career, I tried to make good use of these unforgettable impressions. Don't get me wrong: I'm talking about the sound, not the spot under the piano!

I'm convinced that these early experiences shaped my preference for a dense, rich sound, for "full" music over a violin solo, for instance. I might have grown up with cello solos, Bach suites and the like, but I like it more when other sounds – a piano or a string quartet – are added. Just like in Esslingen, when I used to lie under the piano.

When I said I was allowed to stay in the room, this was true up to a point – until nine o'clock, to be precise, when my mother would call: "Bedtime! You have to go to school tomorrow."

My desperate pleas were invariably met with the terse reply: "No, that's enough now!"

That was sheer nonsense, if only because my room was right next to the music room: it would have been acoustically impossible to sleep. To make matters worse – or better – I would press my ear against the wall so as not to miss a single note, so as to fully and completely absorb the structure-borne sound. Luckily my mother never found out – she would have been capable of moving my bed away from the wall. Or, worse yet, of making me change rooms. She certainly would have had it in her. Why is it that parents, out of love and a duty of care, are incapable of seeing what is really going on inside

4. "The name speaks for itself."

their children? This blindness can lead to the fact that one's whole life, these restrictions are mistaken for coldness.

Years later I had a flat in Stuttgart-Feuerbach right above the DIFIA Film sound studio. Every time an orchestra recorded there, I would lie in bed, listening to the music rise through the floorboards, warm and full, its highs muffled. Inevitably, I would be transported back to the musical evenings in Schelztorstrasse, unable to sleep, unable to think of sleep. It didn't bother me. Quite the opposite: at least my tiredness the next day made sense.

I have remained partial to a full sound. When I started making my own music, I always used a vocal doubler to steer clear of individual solo voices, true to the motto: denser and fuller. This has nothing to do with volume or loudness. As strange as it may sound, my dream of creating rich sounds has been a part of me since I was a child.

At the age of five or six I tried to start playing the violoncello. But my hands were too small and too weak for the instrument. To tide me over, I tried the piano. That worked, more or less, but I lost interest as soon as it started to become more difficult. So, I returned to the cello when I was eight and actually came quite a long way – although I already had to contend with my idleness then. I should have practised much more – I had no inkling yet of my gift. Only later did I notice there must have been enough talent at hand – practising was never among my preferred activities.

I learned to play the cello from my father; he was my first and only teacher. This wasn't ideal as he never really had time for me: one hour a week, sometimes only one hour a month. To really make any progress, I should have looked for a new teacher, but there weren't any in Esslingen. Moreover, my father most certainly wouldn't have tolerated it: "Dr Weber's son taking lessons from another teacher!"

After four years in primary school at the Waisenhof School in Esslingen, I had to pass the entrance examination to get into the Georgii Gymnasium, which I did in 1950. Forever etched in my memory of the Waisenhof School, Herr Maier was the most brutal teacher of my entire schooling. If we hadn't memorized something, for example, he would enjoy caning us with the birch, which was very painful. He targeted the hands and buttocks. He perfectly embodied what I still had to find out: you could teach religion, be Protestant, and still be a bastard. What we failed to memorize were passages of Scripture, assigned the previous day. Herr Maier most certainly did not contribute to a thorough knowledge of the Bible. The strange thing was that, at the time, in the 1950s, corporal punishment of this kind was not deemed alarming, not even by the parents. Herr Maier had licence to strike us, unchecked, for years.

Figure 5: Eberhard Weber with his parents and his sister, confirmation photo, 1954

At the Georgii Gymnasium there was a yearly event on the first day of school to welcome new pupils. I suppose that, just like everywhere else, the headmaster must have given a speech – all I can remember is the little school orchestra. It could only have consisted of a few students, perhaps ten violin and cello players. Yet something strange happened to me. I simply couldn't understand why none of my new schoolmates had to fight back tears, like I did. Far from it, in fact: they were horsing around. I was deeply moved by the wonderful music, unaware at this point that it would soon come to define my life.

It wasn't long until I was allowed to join this orchestra. There were only two or three cellists, all students of my father's. No viola, just three or four violins and no horn section: a pure string orchestra. Herr Hoffmann, who was both the music teacher and the orchestra's conductor, regularly gave me an A in music even though I did nothing besides play the cello. He knew I came from a "classical" home and supported me in every possible way. I enjoyed being part of the orchestra because practice sessions would take place before all major and minor festivities, which allowed me to get out of my regular lessons. We only played simple things – Haydn, Telemann. But I was excused from lessons I didn't like: maths, chemistry, physics. Every now and then Herr Hoffmann would bemoan the absence of a lower-pitched instrument in the orchestra. Meanwhile, in one corner of the music room, standing behind the grand piano, there was a contrabass – but no one knew how to play it.

When I turned fifteen, I was forced to admit that my musical taste was veering more in the direction of "contemporary music" – this expression mustn't be confused with later developments in the field of classical music. In the mid-1950s, I discovered my love of another musical genre. Today it would be called rock'n'roll. Please don't get me wrong: I only liked a few of the Bill Haley songs constantly being played on the radio, especially 'Rock Around the Clock', an early boogie-woogie that already had something jazz-like about it. It gave me a first feel for things that were different. The new types of dance that came along with it did not interest me. I've always preferred listening to moving. My first and only dance lesson partner had to put up with me at for-mal dances, where I would disregard any steps we'd learned. Single-mindedly moving towards the stage, the only thing I cared about was listening to the band. It was hopeless. If the band was good, I didn't want to dance; if it was bad, I wanted to dance even less. Obviously, I'm getting muddled here: danc-ing requires rhythm, something that isn't very pronounced in classical music. In jazz there's plenty of it, more than enough. Yet I would recommend rock and pop to those who are willing to move: they are more about "partying" than listening, anyway. When it comes to jazz, please listen: it's worth it. Not always, but often.

This boogie-woogie sequence would define musical events for years to come. In the cabarets of the 1950s and '60s, too, the introduction of the boogie-woogie into vocal numbers became obligatory, as with Günter Neumann and his Berlin Islanders,[5] for example, or the Munich Laughing

---

5. *Berliner Insulaner.*

and Shooting Association.[6] The harmony and rhythm sequences came to symbolize everything modern, cheeky and bold. No cabaret artist could stand still anymore. Mysteriously this later "pseudo-modernity" is still prevalent in some talk-shows on German television. For reasons unknown to me, it was and still is the far north and southeast of Germany that is most susceptible to anything old hat – as are piano amateurs who believe that a bit of pizzazz never hurts. Invariably, they keep pounding out the corny bass accompaniment on their piano with the left hand. Unfortunately, for many years, every time I was asked what instrument I played and said "the bass," this is the bassline that would be imitated – I was not pleased.

When I discovered my love of jazz at fifteen, I had to face the sad fact that the cello was not a suitable instrument. The contrabass, on the other hand, had firmly established itself as indispensable alongside the drums. And one such instrument stood in the music room of the Georgii Gymnasium in Esslingen, untouched.

6. *Münchner Lach- und Schiessgesellschaft.*

4 "A dab hand"

One day I was allowed to take the contrabass home. My music teacher had permitted this, so that I could practise. He had high hopes that I would tonally complement his school orchestra. However, I already had other plans: Bill Haley had roused my interest in something other than classical music.

The first "real" jazz record I ever listened to was by Dave Brubeck. A so-called EP, a small LP with only a few tracks on each side. Unfortunately, it went astray a long time ago. I'm very sorry it's no longer a part of my collection. I would have loved to know what I found so fascinating, what the EP was called, which tracks were on it.

Without the Internet, the opportunities to make enquiries were limited in my youth. I didn't know much about Brubeck, except that he'd studied with the French composer Darius Milhaud. This didn't really help considering that I only knew Milhaud by name – I'd never heard his music. Quick fixes on YouTube were still decades away. Oddly enough, I allowed myself to deem the Brubeckian bass player substandard. In the middle of my pubertal turmoil, my personal *Sturm und Drang*[1] phase, I became convinced that the bassist should be replaced by someone better – and that "someone" should be me.

The next "real" LP was called *Jazz Goes to Junior College*, with Paul Desmond on the alto saxophone, Norman Bates on the bass and Joe Morello on the drums. I must have listened to it hundreds of times, feeling like I was one of them every time I put the record on, imagining myself onstage, dreaming of being Brubeck's bass player.

Yet I knew precious little of jazz and jazz musicians at this stage. I equated quality with popularity. If I'd heard certain names before, I assumed they had to have a certain level of quality – why else would they have become so well-known? Surely, if they weren't any good, you wouldn't be able to buy

---

1. The late eighteenth-century German literary movement known as "Storm and Stress" or "Storm and Urge."

their records. This is the level of naivety with which I listened to all radio programmes.

Soon, however, I claimed the right to decide for myself what I liked and what I didn't. I started resisting automatic reflexes such as, "if it's being played by one of the greats, it's got to be good." I still had to get used to the fact that it often rubbed people up the wrong way when I didn't find everything that was being universally celebrated appealing.

"The greats! And little Weber is putting on airs? Who does he think he is, this snotty little upstart?"

This is what I feared. While I wanted to belong to the community of savvy connoisseurs, I couldn't profess to like recordings that I simply did not. The radio presenter would speak glowingly of historical recordings one had to have heard. Then they would be played – I wouldn't like them. *The Famous Carnegie Hall Concert* with Benny Goodman in 1938, for example. It didn't speak to me. It did swing, but this was a style I didn't count among my favourites. The constant, rhythmic bass drum banging failed to reach me. The double bass, if present at all, was never loud enough. Back then the tones of the bass weren't so important yet: all it had to do was provide a kind of pulse. It didn't matter whether it was the double bass or the bass drum that took over this task. No one was listening anyway.

I was no fan of Mingus and Ellington, either. Many years later, on the occasion of a festival, I was playing in the municipal hall of Heidelberg with my band Colours, when I briefly came into contact with Charles Mingus. We were the first act. Mingus and his band were up next. During our gig I noticed him watching me from the wings. I couldn't hide a certain pride. It wasn't my playing that interested or fascinated him, though. In the break during which the set was being changed, I noticed Mingus talking with Charlie Mariano. Nothing unusual among seasoned musicians. Charlie was Colours' saxophone player. He was very experienced, having played for Stan Kenton and His Orchestra for a long time.

A few days after our encounter in Heidelberg, my phone rang at home. The American English at the other end of the line was hard for me to make out. It took a while until I realized it was Mingus. He'd got my phone number from Charlie and was calling to find out what kind of a bass I was playing and who had built it for me.

In Esslingen, when I was just starting to discover jazz for myself, I wouldn't have dared to dream of one day talking about my instrument with Charlie Mingus. I had to rely on the radio to learn. Anything that even remotely resembled jazz and had a constant bass impressed me. It didn't matter to me yet what type of jazz the ensembles were playing. The only thing that mattered was that it was jazz. All it took to impress me was for there to be a vibraphone, for example. The names of these ensembles are long-forgotten – who still remembers the Walter Geiger Quintet?

In the afternoons there would be short jazz programmes on the radio, seldom longer than half an hour – much to my regret. The highlight of the week was always Erwin Lehn and His South German Broadcasting Dance Music Orchestra. I always hoped for swinging tracks; instead, it was often hits by the likes of Peter Alexander that would get played. Even if he supposedly loved jazz privately, his singing voice never had the X factor that jazz calls for.

One of the best recommendations, in my opinion, was Hazy Osterwald – before he sold out and started singing the midnight tango on TV every Saturday night.

For a long time I played both classical music and jazz. The first time I ever teamed up with a professional bass player, we played the *Trout Quintet* and a Haydn oratorio – there were two instruments to the part. My professional colleague told me: "You play the recitative, and I'll do the rest." It was only during the rehearsal that I noticed the recitative was the trickiest part for the bass – my professional colleague had been looking forward to a quiet evening. Everything went well regardless.

Opposing factions regularly clashed in my youth, one accusing the other of stuffiness. While one side would say, "Conservative! Old-fashioned!" the other exclaimed, "New-fangled!" For a long time, they seemed irreconcilable.

At some point I stopped wanting to play classical music. I simply lacked the will and the passion. Today I sometimes ask myself if I would have been able to break through in the classical music genre, too, or if I would have gone under in the vast sea of competing musicians. The repertoire was too regimented for me, with real improvisation neither required nor desired. To this day, what appeals to me in art is individuality more than technical perfection. Take Miles Davis, for example: he was no perfect trumpeter, but unlike many of his mind-blowing colleagues, who could only impress with their amazing technique, he developed a style of his own. In jazz, individuality counts more than technical perfection and the pinnacle of individual freedom is reached through improvisation. In classical music you can't change anything. Written phrases have to be played the way you see them on the page. In spite of this, classically trained musicians insist that there is a huge range of variation.

Later in the course of my career, I had the opportunity to play with Friedrich Gulda, the great classical pianist. He was a superstar: even today, his Beethoven and Mozart interpretations are still held up as the gold standard. To the dismay of most classical music concertgoers, he absolutely refused to hide the fact that he was a huge jazz fan. As such, he repeatedly tried to gain ground and recognition in the jazz scene. The dismay of classical music fans was rooted in the fact that Gulda used every opportunity to follow his own inclinations. He did not shy away from incorporating his own cadences into classical piano concerts, from "jazzing up" cadences by playing triplets, for example. Integrating these "jazzy" versions into old music took courage: contemporary perceptions of how to play were connected with old music. It's no wonder that Gulda wasn't met with open arms – he was eaten alive.

This courage appealed to rebels like us back then. At the very least, we were impressed by the clarion call that had been sounded in the sphere of traditional classical music. Friedrich Gulda loved scandal; he wanted to provoke. He actually managed to find favour with jazz fans. We liked him. All the same he was never fully integrated into the scene; despite his phenomenal technique and his theoretically unlimited possibilities, he was no jazzman. I often asked myself why that was. Was it his technique? Was there too much of it? This would mean that average technique is better suited to the jazz musician. When you come to think of it, there were and still are phenomenal "technicians" in jazz, too – Art Tatum, for example. It's got to have something to do with feeling, the delicate feel for this very special music, for improvisation, for creating in the moment.

A Russian pianist, a true titan of technique, was once followed around by a German TV crew on one of his global tours. His name wasn't familiar to me then and I have since forgotten it. He was considered one of the most accomplished pianists when it came to playing difficult pieces fast. It was true: what I heard and saw could have been played by a piano computer programmed to play two or three times as fast as usual: absolutely breathtaking! After one of the maestro's concerts in New York, the TV crew followed him to a jazz club, where he joined the band. What this brilliant technician produced there was indescribable... rubbish! Things are different today – in many classical orchestras there are musicians who move between genres with great ease: jazz, hip-hop, ethno, rock. The world really has become a bit freer in the last sixty years.

Back to Esslingen: I was fixated on jazz. Nothing else interested me. Rock'n'roll didn't do it for me. In dance lessons I refused to learn the steps to new dances like the twist. At the Georgii Gymnasium I met Martin Schwäble, who played the piano and became one of my best friends. Martin was a year ahead of me and played in one of the various school bands – all of them leaning towards jazz: rock hadn't been discovered yet. A drummer and a clarinettist were also part of this band, or "combo," as it was known back then. A fourth pupil played – everything was possible – the accordion. What was missing? A bass player!

During a matinee at the Gymnasium, on the occasion of a celebration for some dignitary, I was "discovered" when I surprisingly appeared in the school orchestra with the bass instead of the cello. If I was walking around with a bass, surely, I must fit the bill for a combo, too.

Yet my career almost took a very different path. When I was still playing the cello in the school orchestra, Herr Hoffman once said: "We've decided to acquire a new instrument. It's going to be a bassoon. Does anybody here want to learn the bassoon?"

I raised my hand immediately. But this bassoon was never purchased, not in my time at any rate. Who knows: if the school had bought a bassoon,

perhaps I would have played the saxophone instead of the bass – one of those alleged accidents of fate that shape life.

Martin Schwäble was not the only band leader at our school – soon I was beleaguered by all the other bands missing a bass. I chose Martin and his crew, though, or rather, initially at least, I chose one particular composition: 'Lullaby of Birdland' by George Shearing. This led me to Lausch & Zweigle, the sheet music store in Stuttgart, to ask: "Do you have printed music for 'Lullaby of Birdland'?" (They did.)

Figure 6: Martin Schwäble and Eberhard Weber at a private event, 1958/59

You can see how important this was for me because I can still remember that the score was published by Chappell Press, a rather trivial detail for all intents and purposes. It was the piano edition, so the right hand played the melody and the left the harmonies and bass accompaniment. That was exactly what I was looking for! These bass notes, long since learned by heart, have accompanied me ever since, time and time again. For those who want to know: a-a F sharp-F sharp B-B e-e, at least in the first two bars. Lower-case letters stand for "minor," uppercase letters for "major." I know this now – back then I was still unencumbered by such facts. Although I knew what the difference between minor and major was, it was still a mystery to me how this should be applied in practical and improvisational terms. I had no idea how to improvise yet. How was this supposed to work? And on a double bass at that? In the end my ears helped me more than any examples on paper. My main asset was my ability to hear, to notice and instantly react to sudden changes of harmony and errors or mistakes made by the other players.

During our first rehearsal, I gradually became aware of the sacrifices the bass demands of a player's uncalloused fingertips. When a jazz player nonchalantly plucks notes to life pizzicato-style with his right hand, it sounds and looks cool. For unpractised fingers, however, this plucking is a real ordeal. Within two or three minutes, blisters start to form, and before you know it, they're filled with some sort of protective fluid, first yellowish, then green or dark red – a Technicolor dream. Too bad that it hurts like hell! No wonder, when you have to keep hitting the same sore spot. Bear in mind that our fingertips are equipped with incredibly sensitive nerve endings that weren't made to tear away at a couple of steel strings. To make matters worse, the contrabass isn't one of the louder unamplified acoustic instruments. So, while the piano and the drums heedlessly assert themselves, the bass player beside them defends himself by exerting more force. One finger after the other capitulates, forming a defence blister. I didn't want the first rehearsal to end early just because of my fingers. What's more, I wanted to be a bass player. So, I used one finger after the other, plucking away with my index, my middle finger, my ring finger and my little finger. Then the thumb and, at last, the knuckles. It's awful how skin will keep defending itself, reacting with pain. I could hardly sleep that night: every beat of my heart caused the blood in the blisters to throb.

After the better half of a year, my fingers finally stopped forming fresh blisters, so that pain-free, and thus more creative pizzicatos became possible. That's how long it takes for the underlying tissue to get accustomed to this unfamiliar strain. During my fifty-year career, I had to come to terms with the fact that, in my case, this habituation of the fingers remained specific to individual instruments: every time I grabbed an instrument that wasn't my own, new blisters threatened to cause more pain. My fingers remained extremely sensitive throughout my career and couldn't endure radical treatment of any kind. I was pain-free, but any new demand on them – a new fingerboard, a new string gauge – represented a risk.

Having memorized the bassline of 'Lullaby of Birdland,' I repeated it stupidly, over and over, without any variation, still clueless and very naïve. I was desperate for the help of a professional.

One afternoon, during one of our frequent rehearsals in the school music room, the door opened and the hoped-for pro walked in: I still remember his name, but why mention it? He was a member of a dance and entertainment music ensemble, and as far as I was concerned back then, he was a seasoned professional: hats off! I firmly believed I could learn something from him, but it was Martin Schwäble who first had the courage to ask him: "Do you know 'Lullaby of Birdland'?"

"Of course!"

"Will you play it with us?"

I was very curious to hear what a professional would sound like. I was shocked: he failed to hit a single note! I noticed this despite not yet knowing which notes were available. I couldn't believe that a pro would play such utter rubbish! But he did: a little "boom-boom" seems to be the only thing that was required of bass players back then.

We would have loved to have lessons and go to a jazz school, but there weren't any yet. As young musicians, our only choice was to learn through our own research and experimentation. There were plenty of opportunities to play. Every town, even the smallest, had a jazz club – usually in a damp cellar that matched the stereotypical life of a jazz musician modelled in Paris by existentialists in black turtlenecks and duffle coats. What a blessing for young people today: colleges everywhere. *Tempora mutantur.*[2] Yes, I did learn Latin at school. And yes, I have personally experienced that change is inevitable.

Anyway, back in my day, bass players had to live up to rather modest expectations. In our music jargon we called it "playing on track" along the lines of: "Would you like it a fist higher?" All that mattered was that you plucked around a little. That's all it took. On top of that the harmonics of many songs were very simple. Precise bass tones seemed secondary: it was enough if the drummer tapped along to the beat on the bass drum. "Boom-boom" was plenty. Since then, harmonies have turned into delicate constructs which the wrong bass accompaniment has the power to distort or destroy.

The measly set of skills I had acquired in the school jazz band grew rather quickly. Soon I was competent enough to earn a few extra Deutschmarks by playing dance music. I was the first one in our band to be asked: bass players were a scarce commodity even among "professionals."

It was New Year's Eve. I was seventeen years old and still living at my parents' when the phone rang that afternoon. I still remember the number: 34 74 89. Could I help out in the evening? The bass player had dropped out and since it was New Year's Eve, a prestigious band had been scheduled to impress the guests. I was stunned – and accepted immediately. The time and place were agreed on. Then I started to think about how I would get to the venue, an inn called Zum Jägerhaus: it was on a hill, it was winter, I would be carrying a double bass without a case, and I had neither a driving licence nor a car. Unimaginable today!

---

2. From the Latin phrase "*tempora mutantur, nos et mutamur in illis*," meaning: "The times change, and we change with them."

I had barely put down the receiver and thought of a way of getting to the inn, when the phone rang again. It was the same caller: "I'm sorry, my colleague has found a replacement since we talked."

All of this excitement and anticipation for nothing. Just before the start of the event the phone rang again: "The replacement for the bass player's slipped on the ice and broken his leg. Are you still available?"

"Yes, I'll be right there."

I put on something dark, shouldered the naked bass, skidded a few hundred metres to the bus stop and squeezed myself onto the crowded bus, which worked out quite well since people spontaneously made way for the unfamiliar gigantic instrument. Half an hour later I was at the Jägerhaus. Two men were waiting there, one accordionist and one guitarist, curious to see what chance was throwing their way.

I didn't need to unpack my bass, so we started playing a few notes immediately and managed to find some sort of agreement before the first guests arrived. I was fully capable of reading music thanks to my early schooling on the cello. But there was no music to read: the two musicians had memorized it. They said it wasn't difficult, and all I had to do was listen carefully. I was used to that sort of thing by then and had already developed a decent routine.

When the guests arrived, the innkeeper greeted them and a few fake noses were distributed to brighten the mood. Then: "*Musik marsch*!" He wasn't expecting a march. "*Marsch*" just means, "Let's get started!"

After a short prelude of only four bars, the first piece: "Tour in F Major" without a score, just by ear. "Tour in F Major" was no hit – it was just a series of old hits in F major. I can recall '*Abends in der Taverne*'[3] and '*Wenn der weiße Flieder wieder blüht.*'[4] The "Tour in F Major" must have lasted around fifteen minutes. I tried my hardest to make a good impression. After all, no one knew who I was yet. After the final note, the dancers provided the obligatory, bored applause on their way back to their tables. I reckoned I had duly completed the task – far from perfectly, but decently. What comments could I expect from the two professionals now? They played at bigger events and dances every Saturday, so I had managed to find out their names. The accordionist, Adolf Wagenseil, turned to the guitarist, Arno Kissler, and said, in heavily accented Swabian: "You know what, I think we've found a dab hand!"[5]

Both were Swabian, like me. When it was all over, astronomic sums of money were handed out: one hundred marks for each of us – for eight hours of dance music, from eight o'clock in the evening to four o'clock in the morning. A lot of money in 1957! Wait! It was after midnight by then, so: 1958!

---

3. "At Night in the Tavern."
4. "When the White Lilac Blooms Again."
5. '*Du, I glaub, do hen mir a Fässle g'fonda!*'

Figure 7: Arno Kissler, Eberhard Weber and Adolf Wagenseil at Weber's first paid public appearance (100 Deutschmarks) on 31 December 1957 at the inn Zum Jägerhaus, Esslingen

It soon became clear that the two of them were hoping to work with me again. But I wanted to play jazz, not popular *Schlager*.[6] So my first choice remained my friend Martin's school band. Things were definitely more "happening" there.

By our own standards, we were tremendously successful, initially as a trio consisting of Martin on the piano, Roland Wittich on the drums (Roland was another friend from school) and myself on the borrowed bass from the Georgii Gymnasium. We had found access to Esslingen's "high society." This included the "glass roof" Eberspächers and the "sauerkraut" Hengstenbergs – to name but a few of the names that were known beyond the boundaries of our little state. The sobriquet stood for their company's main product. We played at their parties and events, and every weekend we performed in the hall of our favourite restaurant, Alte Reichsstadt, right next to the new townhall of the Free Imperial Town of Esslingen am Neckar. This is where people would get married and celebrate their birthdays, and we had become the house band. Over the years we must have played at about 200 weddings. On the most important day in people's lives we witnessed all sorts of things: blissfulness, tears, slideshows, awkward poetic endeavours, laughter, bearskins, speeches, shaky voices, bride kidnappings and a brawl between two

6. Sentimental ballads with a simple, catchy melody and lyrics that often focus on love, relationships or feelings. The literal translation of *Schlager* is "(musical) hit(s)."

enemy clans. Depending on the number of guests, we sometimes had to hire additional musicians, either to play more loudly – there weren't any amplifiers yet – or to signal greater prestige.

Occasionally our trio, The Jobbers as we called ourselves, played with other amateurs. I still remember a saxophone-playing hatter who would sneak into the guest cloakroom during breaks to "work" on the men's hats – perfectly ordinary accessories back then. The hats were slightly oval in shape, tapered at the front with two little dents there. Workmanlike, our hatter knew how to shift the dents to the back, so that the hats wouldn't fit properly anymore. At the end of the evening we would grin inanely when none of the men managed to put on their hats: nobody noticed that the dents were on the wrong side, which probably had something to do with the large quantities of alcohol consumed. Not a single hat fit as it should have. A belated boyish prank – unforgotten for this very reason.

In the area around Stuttgart there were many different dance music bands, ranging from very stuffy ensembles to seriously swinging formations and top acts, usually enriched by soloists from the South German Broadcasting Dance Music Orchestra of Erwin Lehn. A new pianist had emerged there: Horst Jankowski. It was immediately obvious that he was immensely talented. On the other hand, there was something missing as far as I was concerned. Jakob, that's what Jankowski's friends called him, loved the spectacular, the crude – he was already on a quest for success that didn't do his dexterity any favours. Success did come to him: it's certainly fair to say as much after his global hit 'Eine Schwarzwaldfahrt'.[7] But it didn't serve his piano playing well. While there definitely were fast passages, there weren't any that one might have called dazzling or elegant. It wasn't uncommon for his hands to cramp up after he'd finish playing: he tried to showcase too much, to prove himself too often. The fact that he had no critics, and only admirers – us included – most likely didn't help him. I was only able to recognize these details later, when he asked me to play with him – on rare occasions. I also asked myself why, in the world of jazz in particular, there wasn't more of a buzz about him. The expression "dog and pony show" comes to mind.

'Eine Schwarzwaldfahrt' probably could have set him up for life. Unfortunately, for want of money, he had sold the rights too soon, probably making no more than a few hundred marks. A much later attempt to receive a more substantial sum on the legal basis of disproportionality was rewarded, but the compensation amounted to just a few tens of thousands of marks: sold is sold.

Sometimes, our combo managed to invite one of these high-profile musicians, a member of the revered SDR Stuttgart dance orchestra. We were proud: no other small dance music band had managed to do this. Soon I had enough connections to contact even the greats: Horst Fischer and Ernst Mosch. But

7. "A Ride Through the Black Forest."

neither of them ever had any time for us – with good reason. That left the saxophonists of the SDR Stuttgart dance orchestra – they were willing to play even if Fischer and Mosch weren't. Only once did I manage to put together the ultimate line-up, for the formal dance marking the end of my dance lessons: Horst Fischer, trumpet; Ernst Mosch, trombone; Gerald Weinkopf, saxophone; Horst Jankowski, piano; Peter Witte, bass, and Hermann Mutschler, drums. That was almost half of the Erwin Lehn Big Band. A dream line-up! I was even allowed to join in on one occasion: the bass player invited me to use his instrument. I was permitted to prove that I had diligently learned the craft. Jankowski even made room for a bass solo. I was seventeen or eighteen years old and I was playing with my idols. I was bursting with pride. When I eventually got off the stage, I did so slowly, casually, to show everyone where I really belonged… "Now you know who you're looking at…"

Some of the big names, like Ernst Mosch, for instance, later moved on: Mosch, an outstanding trombonist, realized that his earnings from playing traditional folk music with his Original Egerländer Musikanten far surpassed those with Lehn. Under these circumstances it was easy to let jazz be jazz. Keep in mind that Lehn's orchestra only rarely played real jazz, bound by its role as a "dance music orchestra."

Several members of Lehn's orchestra also played in Mosch's early brass orchestra – another reason for the massive success of the Original Egerländer. Ernst Mosch and his orchestra provided the precision that had hitherto been lacking in well-known brass orchestras. It's hard to imagine that you could make it to Carnegie Hall and collect gold records with traditional German folk music. Bernd Rabe, the lead alto saxophone and clarinet player, was also on board at the beginning. He once told me that he was so ashamed of the traditional costume they all had to wear, that he would put on a long coat to hide the ridiculous knee breeches every time he left his flat. Only onstage, in front of the appropriate audience, did he shed his inhibitions.

Horst Fischer, the star trumpeter, followed a different career path. He became "the man with the golden trumpet." He, too, sold "enough" records, was passed around from one celebrated orchestra to the next, appeared on TV shows, and earned good money – until he suffered a terrible fall from grace. He died young, an impoverished alcoholic. There were amazing stories about him that proved his exceptional talent as a trumpeter. On one occasion, Fischer was asked to play the trumpet part of a Bach cantata. Astonished, the conductor noticed that the soloist had brought a regular trumpet to the rehearsal even though the cantata called for a so-called Bach trumpet, a much smaller instrument that makes it easier to play high notes. This was not a problem for Horst Fischer. He played all the high tones on his regular trumpet with virtuosic ease. "I'll bring the Bach to the performance, then." That was Horst Fischer.

At one point I got the chance to stand in for my idol of the time, the bass player of the SDR dance orchestra, Peter Witte, nicknamed Fifi. This is how

I gained first-hand experience of day-to-day life in a professional orchestra. I arrived early in the large broadcasting hall of Villa Berg, the studio of the Erwin Lehn Orchestra, and while I was warming up, my older colleagues arrived one after the other, greeting me warmly. They already knew me and seemed pleased that I was there. I was still firmly convinced then that professionals were anxious to play good music – especially in this incredible line-up.

The bass parts of two compositions already rested on my music stand – my task for the four-hour recording session (from ten in the morning to two in the afternoon). I studied them carefully, so as not to be conspicuous once we got started. There were no extravagant arrangements. The conductor, Erwin Lehn, arrived, also greeting me warmly. He'd been informed that there would be a replacement. He already knew me, which caused him to grant me some freedom, urging me not to stick to the notes. That was just what I'd been waiting for! To finally be able to show how modern bass was played! After the first recording, Erwin Lehn came over to me and said: "Very nice, Herr Weber! Really great! But a bit less next time, please."

Surely my youthful drive had led me to overdo it a bit. Lehn's request must have been fully justified. But after the next take, he had exactly the same reaction – although I had consciously shown real restraint.

In the end, Lehn asked me to play only the notes that were printed. That's the recording that was finally used.

When it came to the second piece, I just played the prescribed notes from the start. Right off the bat, everything was just perfect!

After the two recordings were made, I watched on with amazement as the other musicians hurriedly packed up their instruments and Lehn dismissed them: "Gentlemen, see you tomorrow!"

Tomorrow? There were two whole hours left! Giving voice to my astonishment, I was wise enough to whisper when I asked the alto saxophonist, Bernd Rabe, why we weren't recording more compositions if there was so much time left. "Are you mad?" he replied. "Then we'd have to record that much every day!"

As an amateur, I wanted to do nothing but play, play, play…

As a professional, there was nothing I wanted more than to go home. Well… I was still an amateur.

It would have made sense for me to go to the arts Gymnasium in Stuttgart, but my mother refused: "By train? So far away? All alone? I'd worry the whole time!"

Imagine that: I couldn't make my dream come true because she was afraid. So I stayed at the Gymnasium in Esslingen until, at last, I reached the final year. Even then, though, I devoted all my time to music. I just didn't get round to studying for the *Abitur* exam. Initially I'd done very well in my classes, then just well, then just well enough. Towards the end, it got tough. During the last three years at the latest, I should have started preparing for my exams – yet I spent most of my time on my obsession, listening to music, ultimately just to jazz. What had to happen did happen: I failed the *Abitur* and was escorted home by a teacher of religious education – probably because it was rumoured that other "offenders" had committed suicide. My attempts to discourage the teacher remained unsuccessful. He didn't leave until we reached my home and I unlocked the front door. My father had been waiting and looked at me enquiringly. I simply shook my head. My father's memorable reaction: "What is this going to make me look like?"

Doctor Weber's son had failed the *Abitur*! He projected massive guilt onto me. In the following weeks, I barely dared leave the house, believing all of Esslingen would point at me, whispering: "He failed!" I stayed at home, varnished all the doors and windows several times over, leaving the flat only briefly to buy more varnish. Luckily the paint shop, Farben-Leins, was just a few meters away.

These were dreadful weeks for me. During my entire childhood I had been systematically raised to get a "steady" job one day. My mother wouldn't even have minded if I'd become a parson. Not that she was particularly religious. "Steady employment!" was her shibboleth. Who cares who pays as long as someone pays – your whole life long! This was completely incompatible with the life my father was leading, a musician's life. My father had "only" made it as far as private music teacher. No life-long pension. No sick pay. Paid holidays? God forbid. Endless risks! Her son should have it easier! He should be anything but a musician. "Get a proper education," they say. "Something sensible,"[8] says the Swabian.

For those who care to know, I had been enrolled at Esslingen's teacher training college to become a primary school teacher. This plan had to be abandoned now. Actually, I should have been happy, but far from it. My upbringing had radically banned thoughts of this nature. The idea that parents could be wrong was alien to me then. The end of my schooling was disappointing, especially for my parents. Doctor Weber's son had failed his exams and wasn't prepared to spend another year at the Gymnasium. The Esslingen chapter was over as far as I was concerned. A new one had to begin.

---

8. *"Was G'scheits!"*

5 "Hey, how about it?"

What's the story with Wolfgang Dauner, the great German pianist, my first mentor? When and why did we meet? Neither of us can remember. It must have been sometime around 1960. We both had obligations – he was studying music in Stuttgart, I'd landed in commercials. Yet I'd been dreaming of a career in music for a long time. But I was sick and tired of studying and school. In order to get a steady job, I wanted to do an apprenticeship. Film and television appealed to me. How to get taken on in the field of television, though? My sister was already working in the sound archive of SDR Stuttgart, and her husband knew every Tom, Dick and Harry. He explained to me that training as a photographer would be a good basis for a job in television. So, off to Esslingen's Foto-Claus[1] I went!

Now things got boring: wedding photos and passport photos from morning to evening. Developing, enlarging, retouching. But after I completed my apprenticeship as a photographer, my brother-in-law really was able to help. He was now Horst Jankowski's lyricist and, as such, opened the door to the film business for me. Horst Jankowski, in turn, knew a certain Rolf Winkler, who was active in the field of commercials with his company DIFA. DIFA also ran a handful of cinemas in Stuttgart. And Herr Winkler, a jazz lover, liked the idea of having a talented young musician in his company. I became assistant to the executive producer. I was over the moon. I was working "in film" and, at the same time, still had plenty of time to work as a jazz musician. What more could you ask for at that age.

At that time I became a member of the Horst Jankowski Singers. This choir came into being in the 1960s, at the time of the Ray Coniff Singers, who were always on the radio. "We could try something like that in Germany,

---

1. Professional photographer's shop/studio.

Figure 8a: Eberhard Weber (with Martin Schwäble as his model) during his apprenticeship as a photographer in 1959

Figure 8b: Eberhard Weber as a camera assistant during the shooting of a commercial for Swissair on the coast of Beirut (Lebanon), 1962

Figure 9: Eberhard Weber on tour in Russia with the Horst Jankowski Singers in August 1968. Centre: Ludmilla (translator); to her right: Roland Wittich

too!" Jankowski thought to himself. He was successful. You didn't need to be a trained vocalist to join the Jankowski Singers. In fact, your voice was secondary as long as you didn't have any ambitions as a soloist. The main issue was whether you had accurate intonation. I did have that – even if my voice rather resembled the croaking of my father. In a choir, a lot of things go unnoticed as long as one bows to the music and doesn't just "bellow" loudly. I ended up appearing on Jankowski's TV shows every couple of Saturdays with his Singers – mostly interested amateurs, and a handful of professional musicians. There were shows like *Sing with Horst*, for instance, but also the big Saturday night entertainment shows of Peter Frankenfeld, Hans-Joachim Kulenkampff and Joachim Fuchsberger. One of our few guest appearances took us to the Soviet Union – all the way to St. Petersburg.

By this stage I'd met Wolfgang Dauner's regular bass player, Götz Wendland. One day Götz invited me to one of the trio's gigs – they played covers, like all bands did in the early 1960s. Most of the songs were well-known or should have been well-known. In the course of the evening, Götz asked me to step in at one point, which I did immediately – my heart was pounding. It went well. A few days later, the telephone rang at home: "Listen, Götz isn't available. Can you take his place?"

I could – and that was the end of Götz's membership in the Wolfgang Dauner Trio. I assume that the way I played was more modern. There must have been something about it that impressed Dauner. Looking back, Götz Wendland may actually have been happy about this turn of events – he, too, was a "Jankowskian." He later played the bass on Jankowski's famous *Schwarzwaldfahrt*, and established himself in the entertainment industry. Among other things, he was in charge of the music for Hans Rosenthal's popular TV show *Dalli Dalli*, for a couple of years.

An old story of his made quite an impression on me at that young age. On tour for Maggi – the instant noodle and seasonings company – he had his fee paid in tins of ravioli. I can confirm it: the tins filled his pantry from floor to ceiling. I, too, once had to consume the contents of one of these tins, camouflaged as "lunch." He really must have been a huge fan of ravioli, eating out of a can for months on end.

What interested me about Wolfgang Dauner's Trio was the chance to learn from his musical experience. While I had achieved local recognition as an amateur by then, Wolfgang had long been a professional. He had all sorts of engagements of which he spoke often. It wasn't always art for the sake of art – the price had to be right, too. That's why he regularly played at a nightclub in Stuttgart, accompanying the strippers' stimulating contortions. I was surprised to find out that he had originally studied to become a trumpeter and still played the trumpet with other bands – even in a formation that went on tour with Marika Rökk. The 1968 student movement was still light years away…

This reminds me of a wonderful anecdote of Wolfgang's dating back to that time. He was on tour with an MC one winter, and as it tends to go with jobs of this sort, it doesn't take long for the band to know every joke and every punchline. One evening, the band had managed to fight its way through the snow, but the MC was stuck somewhere. What could they do? One of the musicians volunteered to assume the role of MC, and the show started on time as planned. Things followed their usual course, and the audience enjoyed the witticisms of the stand-in. After the intermission, the original MC finally arrived, out of breath and annoyed. But when he got onstage to take over the second half of the show, he could make neither head nor tail of the audience's reaction: first, he was laughed at, then he was booed. No wonder: the substitute MC had deliberately told the jokes of the second half of the show in the first half. Management did not approve – the prankster was fired.

Figure 10: Fritz Dautel, Theo Lippmann, Achim Leinstoll and Eberhard Weber at the American Club in Nellingen, 1960

Back then it was perfectly normal to play all over the place: in nightclub A, in café B, in the barracks of "the *Ami*" with band C or sextet D. To boot, the boundaries between jazz and *Schlager* were porous. My engagements were similar to those of Wolfgang. I may not have toured with Marika Rökk, but I did with Conny Froboess, just known as Conny back then. I had a huge crush on the teen idol, but never made a move – I was still too shy. Besides, her father was always nearby, chaperoning her. The reason I was on tour with her in Switzerland at all had to do with a certain Gerhard Wehner Ensemble. A few weeks earlier, I had been uncharacteristically late – very late – on the occasion of a radio production with Bibi Johns and ... Gerhard Wehner. I owed him one and he booked me for the tour with Conny. Decades later I met Bibi Johns again after a concert at the Cologne Philharmonic Hall, where I had played a short solo in honour of Manfred Schoof's birthday. We laughed at the memories, which were now forty years old.

I played with Wolfgang Dauner for ten years, and we got along brilliantly, not just in terms of music. I helped him varnish the bathroom of his aging terraced house in Stuttgart-Münster – after all I was experienced. I even painted a perfectly straight dividing line on the wall. In return, Wolfgang helped paint the toilet in my parents' home. Musically we started with the usual sets: melody, chorus, chorus, chorus, melody. Applause, next song. Then, inevitably, the ballad. We'd get through it quickly, so that we could continue up-tempo. A medium blues, maybe?

One big problem was finding a drummer. For a while, a certain Siggi Knispel filled the position, with little success. At times he would develop bizarre ideas. Apparently, he was seriously considering blinding himself because his big idol, the Dave Brubeck drummer Joe Morello ("Take Five"), was blind. To keep it short: we looked for other drummers, didn't find anyone for a long time and heard at some point that Knispel had become an alcoholic and died shortly thereafter.

Figure 11: The Wolfgang Dauner Trio in the early 1960s with Fred Braceful, Eberhard Weber and Wolfgang Dauner

For some time, we played as the Wolfgang Dauner Duo. Our shrinking trio was successful: we were repeatedly invited to Esslingen's jazz club, the Jazzkeller. Though fascinating, this was not an architecturally enticing cellar: damp, stuffy, smoky, accessible only via steep, narrow wooden stairs, and it didn't have any toilets! To do one's business, one had to find a quiet corner outside – unimaginable today. Yet renowned musicians appeared at the club on a regular basis and played their hearts out. These were transformative years. What worked in Paris and Copenhagen had to be possible in Esslingen, too! Interesting random fact: to this day the Jazzkeller is located on Webergasse…

One evening Wolfgang and I were giving a new drummer a go in this cellar when a member of the audience, an African American guy from the army, asked if he could take a crack at it. The drums were set up, so, yes! That's how we found our solution: Fred Braceful! Fred played exactly to our taste. He was modern, a bit like Elvin Jones, the drummer of the John Coltrane Quartet – totally different from all German drummers put together. He didn't cling to convention. I called the traditional way of playing "Dubcec-du-Dubcec" with a hi-hat on two and four – to this day all swing drummers still play this way. The only problem was that apart from Wolfgang and me, no one liked Fred's unconventional style: "He doesn't swing! He's got no technique."

Although no one shared our point of view, we remained convinced. The conventional way of playing just wasn't Fred's thing. He was a little Elvin Jones. No "Dubcec-du-Dubcec" groove with a hi-hat on two and four. Marvellously different in spite of his deplorable technique, which Wolfgang and I certainly noticed. Someone once put it like this: "An outstanding musician. Unfortunately, also a poor drummer!"

In the realm of the bass there were several shining examples. First, I noticed Paul Chambers, who had played with a young Miles Davis for a while. I found it unusual that he often omitted the root note in his line without anyone ever noticing or missing it. To my ear this created a sort of lightness.

Paul Chambers was known, but he was never as famous as Ray Brown, who influenced my taste next. He was Oscar Peterson's accompanist in the legendary trio with Ed Thigpen on the drums. They really made my heart sing! They could swing like devils. I'm afraid that for a while I may have tried to imitate Ray Brown.

I had firmly resolved not to do this with any of my idols, but I found some of Ray Brown's phrases and passages truly exceptional. So why not copy them? Why not use them? The listener certainly wouldn't notice. The sound quality of Brown's bass was completely different from that of my own 210 Deutschmark creation. No one would ever imagine that the sequences of notes were the same!

And so, we, too, went through the Oscar Peterson Trio phase: great foot-tapping, bouncing swing. One day Wolfgang said, "Hey…" (Wolfgang started most sentences with "Hey.") "Hey, I've got tickets to go see Oscar!"

Ecstatic, we sat in the first row of the Gustav-Siegle-Haus in Stuttgart. The trio was playing, with Ray Brown on bass, and Ed Thigpen on drums. I had just bought the band's new record and listened to every piece over and over again. Sheer madness!

Right at the beginning of the concert they played my favourite piece. I was in seventh heaven. I could have sung along, just like on the record. The prelude was over, then the melody, twice, the middle section, the melody again, break and... What was happening?

Peterson played completely differently from the way he did on the record! It took me a while to realize: "They're improvising!" At that moment, for the first time, I felt the discrepancy that many people in the audience experience time and time again – between wanting to hear one's favourite piece the way one already knows it on the one hand, and being strangely fascinated with the freedom and creativity of improvisation on the other hand.

The next giant leap – or, rather, giant break – came when I discovered an entirely new way of accompanying on a double bass, inspired by the great, exceptional bass player of the Bill Evans Trio, Scott LaFaro. With him on the bass and Paul Motian on the drums, Evans created a totally new perspective on jazz. You could forget any attempt at imitating Scott LaFaro. For the standards of the time, he played so incredibly well – he was technically unparalleled – that the lunatics who tried to imitate him always ran the risk of being exposed as cheap copies. LaFaro alone – and no one else – could play like this! In his solos he romped about in the higher realms of the range, and where others played a traditional walking bass, he developed his very own counter melodies. Sadly, he died in a car accident in 1961, the same year the legendary *Sunday at the Village Vanguard* session and *Waltz for Debbie* were recorded. Scott was just twenty-five years old.

Wolfgang Dauner liked my "crazy discovery." I was just confused because he'd already made the discovery before me. Why hadn't he told me? He just said: "Hey, then we can play other things now!"

The new Dauner Trio became really successful and stayed together. In 1964 we made a terrific LP, *Dream Talk*, which unfortunately isn't available anymore. Horst Lippmann, a producer and partner of the music agency Lippmann and Rau, had produced it under conditions that are hard to imagine today. He'd rented the studio of the Erwin Lehn Big Band, located in a large house called Villa Berg, from seven to eleven in the evening. Everything was already set up when we arrived. We started to play a bit, the producer listened to a few measures, and we were good to go: we played our well-practised programme, piece after piece. After each composition we asked the producer, "How was it?"

"Good – keep going."

By exactly eleven o'clock, all eight compositions were recorded.

"Can we listen to everything now?"

"No. The caretaker has to lock up the studio. He wants to go home."

We were only able to listen to our recording many weeks later when the first test pressing was available. Those were the days!

Scott LaFaro was the last bass player I idolized. Very early on it was all about my own sound, which I never actively sought: it just developed over the years, partly owing to the shortcomings of our equipment, partly to those of my instrument and partly to my own. It all started with the contrabass I'd borrowed from the Gymnasium. Ignorant of jazz, I was fully satisfied with the quality of this instrument. I didn't know anything better and wouldn't have known what to play differently. After I left school, I had to return the bass and buy my own with borrowed money. Out of necessity I bought the cheapest bass I could find in Baden-Württemberg. I got it from Musikhaus Raab in Göpingen for 210 Deutschmarks. A lot of money to me, especially in light of the fact that the bass was unplayable. First, it had to be mended for another two hundred marks by a luthier in Stuttgart called Walter Hamma. I can't recall today what "injuries" the bass had sustained. Apart from the usual cracks in the body, a broken neck would have been particularly serious. A loose neck would have been problematic, too, as this could have led to it breaking very soon. After the repairs I was very satisfied with the quality of my bass's sound. To boot, I had bought a professional case for the first time: now the base was finally portable and protected from scuffs.

The luthier, Hamma, had had a big influence on me since my childhood. I'd first met him right after the war – it must have been around 1946, when I was just six years old. My father always made an instrument available to his younger students until it was clear whether they would stick with it or not. For this purpose he made use of his connection with Hamma. The family business was run by two brothers: one specialized in sales, the other in the repair and making of stringed instruments. Hamma was the European leader as far as top string instruments were concerned. He had encyclopaedic knowledge of famous luthiers and their "oeuvre." To this day his books are standard references. The Hammas, so the legend went, could even unmask thieves. If someone tried to sell them a stolen instrument, they would recognize it at once: "This is the Guarneri that was recently reported as stolen by violinist X."

Although these stories made a big impression on me as a child, this isn't why I'm bringing up the Hamma brothers now. Much more important was the fact that my father brought me with him to Stuttgart every time one of his students wanted to buy a violoncello. This is how, after many tests and trials, I came to hear the difference between a 200, a 400 and an 800 Deutschmark cello – and sometimes, even a cello reaching the astronomical sum of 1000 marks or more. Presumably it wasn't parental love alone that moved my father to bring me along to the Hammas time after time – the fact that his son had young ears that didn't suffer from high frequency hearing loss will also have played a role.

One unique instrument of the Hammas remains etched in my memory: an Amati violoncello with a price-tag of 40,000 Deutschmarks, locked away in a "poison cabinet," waiting to be discovered by a wealthy admirer. Without ever finding one. Why? Because the instrument most definitely wasn't worth that much! Its high price was owed to its illustrious name alone. I could hear that it barely sounded like a 1000 Deutschmark instrument.

Surprises like these also taught me that almost all string instruments have sound defects here and there which are remedied with so-called "wolf tone eliminators," small metal tubes that are placed onto a string between the tailpiece and the bridge. A "wolf" is a weak point that only amplifies a single tone. The tubes are then affixed with a screw to the precise location of the wolf in order to prevent the "wolf tone."

However, "wolf tone eliminator" is an inadequate description as there is no "elimination" to speak of – the unclear sound merely gets shifted. This is how: if, for example, an F that cannot be played properly appears in fourth position on the A string, it can be moved by a couple of millimetres, so that the ugly "wolf tone" is shifted towards the F sharp. Careful, though! It mustn't be shifted all the way to the F sharp, merely in its direction, in compliance with the quarter tones. It is then the player's responsibility to hit either the F or the F sharp – precisely. If the player plays perfectly, the "wolf tone" isn't discernible anymore because quarter tones don't appear in normal literature.

It is incredible how many instruments make use of these "wolf tone eliminators," be they violins, violas or cellos. They are far less common with contrabasses as these don't play as big of a role in classical music. When it comes to pizzicato bass in jazz, this negative effect is virtually impossible to hear.

I am convinced that this early ear training in the Hammas' rooms played a significant role in my later precision, and, therefore, in my career. How many talented young ears have the opportunity to study differences in sound between 250, 310, 480 and 640 mark cellos? Or to shift "wolf tone eliminators" by quarter tones – or, better yet, eighth tones – between the ages of six and fourteen? If this isn't training!

Back to my own 210 mark instrument: I didn't find out until years later that there were better instruments with more optimal action which were easier to play. Wolfgang Dauner asked a colleague – Jürgen Karg, a bass player from the SDR symphony orchestra – to play a high solo tune, A-D-G-C, and this is what first showed me what it means to abandon the "range" of a normal contrabass, E-A-D-G, and to venture into cello realms. His bass only had four strings as well, but they were higher. My wish to press onward and upward took shape then. There was, however, one problem: with higher strings I would be missing the lowest string, the E string. I therefore went to my bass maker and together we tested whether a fifth string could be added to my instrument.

"It might work," he said, "but five strings call for a much sturdier neck in order to withstand the additional strain."

The wood had to withstand the extra tension. It had to be solid and stable enough. I was indifferent to the cost at this point – I just wanted to be able to play higher. A fifth tuning peg was installed in the pegbox, but the four-string fingerboard remained unaltered because I preferred having the strings on the fingerboard closer to each other, like on a cello – in other words: five strings on a four-string fingerboard. Now the trick was to keep the strings as close as possible to the board to lessen the pressure required from the fingers of the left hand. This contributed to a more relaxed, effortless feeling on the one hand, and longer-lasting tones on the other. The bass began to "sing."

When does a bass sound good? When does it swing? When does it just hammer out notes? I introduced the following term for my own purposes: the bass "hums." Slightly buzzing, rasping strings produce a sound of their own, which a bass guitar, for example, isn't capable of. Its sound usually resides in the domain of pure tones – perfect acoustics reign here. If the strings are close enough to the fingerboard, which only works with the fretless model, a somewhat electric rumble is generated, but nothing individual, unfortunately, because electric guitars are hardly capable of developing a life of their own. Four different contrabasses sound different four times over. Four bass guitars of the same type and brand sound the same. It's up to the player to create something different and unique with his phraseology.

The redesign of my bass went well: nothing broke, and the sound became more and more elegant in spite of the low purchase price of my now "beefed up" instrument. You couldn't have found a better bass for less than several thousand marks! I'm not sure if basses with five strings were common in jazz in the past or if mine really was the first. What's certain is that there have always been five-stringed instruments in classical music – even today they are part of every symphony orchestra. Only there, the additional string, the low B, is at the low end. At the top, the G string is the height of pleasure. In my case, however, it was, and still is, the C. So I had a "normal" bass with the option of playing higher, thereby giving myself much more leeway for solos. Building a six-stringed bass, B-E-A-D-G-C, is a dream I preferred to leave in the realm of phantasy. I could, of course, have tried out this even crazier idea with my electric contrabass – I'd even planned to. But fate had something else in store for me.

Now peace had come to stay. My whole life I've only ever had this one contrabass – even now, as I write, it stands beside me in my studio.

Soon, however, the march towards greater volume was underway. And it became clear that in this respect the bass was inferior to all other instruments. In the early 1960s, "electrification" wasn't in full swing yet – the sound quality of pickups and amplifiers was still being developed. Another drawback was that it pains a musician's soul when one tinkers with his beloved wooden instrument, or, worse yet, drives screws into it. Even if he allowed it: Who on earth made such instruments? Would they sound convincing once they were altered? What if the screw holes were made in vain, serving only to disfigure the instrument? The vast quantities of specialized literature available today didn't exist back then. It basically came down to playing guinea pig and hoping for a miracle of sound. Unfortunately, the quality of early amplification options left much to be desired; seen through the lens of youthful naivety and enthusiasm, disappointing results often appeared far better than they really were. All that mattered was being among the first to electrically refashion – or rather, bungle – the old bass tone. At least one could finally be heard without getting muffled by one's colleagues' instruments.

I must have felt a certain degree of dissatisfaction to set out on my quest without yet knowing in which direction it would take me. It was pure chance that one day Wolfgang Dauner saw a strange instrument in the window of a music shop in Stuttgart, basically a board with strings strung across it. He borrowed the odd shrunken bass and brought it to a recording session in the studio: "Hey, see if you can play this!"

Since the position of the strings was similar to that of my own instrument, I saw no reason to refuse, even if there were only four strings. It's downright incredible that I immediately agreed to a recording: we were going to record an LP, and here I was, leaving my favourite bass in its case in favour of this unknown new instrument. The result was nothing stupendous. Still, the new mixture of acoustic and electronic wasn't altogether unpleasant. Like I said, youthful enthusiasm caused one to be open, to try to figure out whether a new instrument of this sort wouldn't lead to something.

These days I've noticed that there are hardly any musicians who don't have their own special instrument, hardly any who would agree to play on an instrument they aren't familiar with. All that these specialists show off is their own specialness. At some point, I became one of them – no question. Once you are locked in place, you lose all interest in the instruments of others. However, when I was still young and naïve, I had the following experience. George Gruntz, the Swiss pianist, invited me to play with him in a trio in a Basel jazz club. I have no idea why I arrived in Basel without a bass. I was aware that there was an opening act, and I wanted to ask the other bass player to lend me his. He wasn't keen. As he handed me his instrument, he said in Swiss German: "A bass player without a bass is bullshit."[2] He was right.

Since the 1970s at the latest, many publications, guitar and bass magazines, have been asking the question: "Who plays what?" It's all about the instrument itself, the number of strings, the pickups, the loudspeakers. I have always been the wrong person to ask in this respect – these questions never mattered much to me. Besides, I'm bothered by the fact that many of these magazines only manage to survive by selling ad space. Consequently, they don't like to report that I have no idea what make of strings I use, how hard or thick they are, or that I don't go through that many. Only when I was still a beginner, eons ago, did it happen that a string would snap – be it through

2. *"Ein Bassischt ohne Bass ischt ein Seich."*

impetuous handling or predetermined breaking points on delicate areas of the instrument, on the nut of the fingerboard or further down at the bridge. Later on, this basically never happened again. As far as the not entirely unimportant amplifiers and devices for additional effects are concerned, I only ever picked them by weight – I never trusted reviews.

One of my earliest bass idols, the previously mentioned Red Mitchell, played on a bass stool into which he had built a loudspeaker, which was also a weight-saving measure. When I met Red somewhere, I spoke about this with the Swedish violinist Svend Asmussen – the two of them travelled and played together. Red was full of praise, but Svend mocked the pitiful sound. Yet they harmonized beautifully with each other and played great little masterpieces. But I admit: weight shouldn't be the only gauge. I was simply very lucky that my weight restrictions ended up not causing any problems. It wasn't until much later, when the equipment was looked after (and schlepped) by our own roadcrew, that I unreservedly devoted myself to the tonal. And lo and behold: the new sound was much better than the old. How had I managed all these years with lighter, less attractive tones?

Still, it was always my own playing that mattered more to me than any technical gimmickry – including strings. I often used the same strings for well over ten years. I never changed them – unimaginable for many a string fetishist. It's important to me to point out that I was never accused of having inadequate equipment. The quality of amps, loudspeakers, strings, reverberators, or delay and chorus devices appears to be utterly insignificant as far as the listener is concerned. Admittedly, this isn't great news for the industry. And even less so for the ambitious beginner, who's got to have nothing but the latest gear. Later on, in the Jan Garbarek Group, there were repeated opportunities to notice remarkable changes. Yet it was always a disappointment for colleagues who believed they were presenting something new and superior: nobody noticed a thing! On one occasion Jan Garbarek secretly played a different saxophone, of a different make. From time to time, he would also try out different mouthpieces. Filled with anticipation, he would direct his gaze at us: "And?"

"And what?"

"You didn't notice anything?"

"What are you talking about?"

Disappointment verging on consternation. My new delay unit and my reverberator suffered the same fate. Neither my colleagues nor the sound crew would pick up on such changes. This is dreadful news for young musicians convinced that this or that device will render a successful career inevitable.

That being said, I have yet to meet a musician who was unreservedly satisfied with his instrument. My cousin, Klaus Schochow, who became a famous classical flautist, spent his entire career moving backwards and forwards between transverse flutes made of wood, silver and gold. Every time, one would be slightly better than the others – until it wasn't anymore. And it can never be ruled out that one's colleagues' instruments won't seem better than one's own. Incidentally, in France, the land of baguette par excellence, everyone makes the same discovery: your neighbour's baguette always tastes better than your own.

"I can't live without my instrument," is a statement I hear again and again. I could never relate to this – I've always lived splendidly without mine! You see, I am of the opinion that breaks are important. Between tours I would only touch my bass when it was time to get going again, and even then, just to toughen up my fingers. You don't unlearn music in just a couple of weeks. After longer breaks, I would take about two weeks to get my fingers reacquainted with the odd procedure for the first concert to go smoothly. The second concert wasn't always fun – my fingers would hurt. After that, the routine of being on tour would set in – adrenaline helped me forget the pain.

But back to Wolfgang Dauner: he was incredibly talented. One of his talents was finding opportunities for us to play. He, too, knew every Tom, Dick and Harry in Stuttgart and the surrounding area. I was surprised how often we got to play – and how many different kinds of places we got to play in, be they art galleries on the occasion of vernissages, or furniture shops luring customers into their salesrooms with the Wolfgang Dauner Trio. Whether this really improved their sales, I don't know.

During my entire time with Dauner, I continued making commercials on the side – or rather, full-time. My boss was happy with my work and proud to be employing an aspiring young jazz musician. And since I displayed a great deal of commitment, volunteering to work overtime without complaining, he repaid me generously and gratefully by letting me go on short tours with the Dauner Trio from time to time. In turn, my employment didn't bother Dauner's circles and soon enough we were playing all over Germany. Sometimes in jazz clubs, at other times in classier establishments. Sometimes with guests such as Manfred Schoof, the two Mangelsdorffs, Jean-Luc Ponty, Pierre Cavalli or Don Menza, and at other times without guests. I only had limited contact with other bands at this time – working with Wolfgang was enough for me. In my opinion, this was one of the high points of his career. His piano playing was exceptional at the time.

In the course of our collaboration, I noticed that Wolfgang was steering his playing in a "freer" direction. The 1968 movement was drawing closer. Many other colleagues were on the same – no, a similar – trip. The Schoofs, Brötzmanns, Schlippenbachs and Mangeldorffs all took a strictly instrumental direction – Dauner and I, on the other hand, while applying all our new acoustic ideas, also enjoyed the "happening." In light of this, Wolfgang procured old violins and guitars for himself, only to spectacularly saw them to pieces onstage. Once, he brought a huge swathe of parachute silk. We disappeared beneath it, moving along to the sounds of chaos typical of the time: scratching, screeching, squeaking.

Soon different fronts were forming: on the one hand, the serious sound-makers; on the other, us, making similar sounds, but evidently not taking this new "freedom" all too seriously – perhaps even poking fun at it. A certain contempt was discernible. We were seen as "nest foulers," fouling our own nest – and that of our colleagues in the other camp.

6 Free!?

The time of the 1968 student movement remains unforgotten. For the good, as well as the questionable. Those who were there felt compelled to participate, regardless of their age. Upheaval took precedence. Protest! Even if it wasn't always clear why or what for; as long as something was happening. Fighting in the streets isn't what I focused on. Instead, it continued to be just music, improvised music, of course, at Wolfgang Dauner's side. But here, too, it was all about breaking with standards, with tradition, about starting something new.

Figure 12: From the left: Wolfgang Dauner, Aldo Romano, Jean-Luc Ponty, Eberhard Weber. Pori, Finland

Back then, anything that couldn't be made "with one's mouth or hands" was categorically forbidden. Electricity or electronics: verboten! The term "jazz," however, was still in use – for ever-freer forms of play, further and further removed from musical structures of any sort. You weren't allowed to count off at the start of a piece, you just began. All known rules were prohibited. Rhythm, harmony, melody – all were banned from free jazz. Jazz does have rules and clear structures, though.

At the beginning, I struggled. This was supposed to be jazz? The expression "free jazz" was settled on. I must admit that from a purely linguistic point of view I preferred this term to the tedious search for other expressions, such as "free play" or "free music." After all, even die-hard Dixieland has-beens claim to be playing jazz. So why shouldn't a "freebooter" call himself a jazz musician?

By then, new, more progressive forms had evolved out of every kind of jazz – until free jazz put an end to this development: "This is as far as it goes!"

How much further could it have gone, anyway, if the final destination was chaos? The only possible solution – and it was implemented – was regression: away from the sophisticated, the individual. Back to the tonal. Free-spiritedness poured its chaos over melodiousness and rhythms. Even today, free players adhere to their achievements. Rhythm and harmonies are accepted – after they are released into a "free" tonal cosmos. Or, rather, after it is blown and hammered into them.

The appellation "jazz" remained ubiquitous. However, once there was talk of a "movement," fierce ideology was brought into play. I did not like this at all, as it went hand in hand with doggedness, intolerance and presumptuousness. Anyone who held on to musical structures was accused of being square. If you dared play anything traditional, or anything new powered by electricity, you were met with derision.

"What, for heaven's sake, does beauty have to do with music? We're in the midst of an upheaval!"

At some point in the early 1960s, I met Albert Mangelsdorff, the figurehead of German jazz. I can't remember where we met, but it must have been at the Esslingen jazz club. I'd just started playing with Dauner, and for the young amateur I was, playing with Albert and his champions was unforgettable. It's difficult for me to definitively state what differentiated the music I played with Wolfgang Dauner from the way Albert and his ensemble played. I guess I preferred our newer way of playing with Dauner to the more "conventional and traditional" interpretations of other German formations. Dauner and I cautiously took a direction I would describe as "elegant."

During the time of the movement of '68, Albert Mangelsdorff, like other formations around Sauer, Schlippenbach and Schoof, for example, was already on a more direct path to hardcore free jazz. And I have to admit, that I, too, initially tried to endorse this radical direction. We happened to be around at the time of the upheaval of '68 – not taking part was out of the question. With the advantage of hindsight, I can now see that I must have done it reluctantly. I took part because it was the done thing.

At the considerable age I am now, I can look back on many ways of playing. It remains impossible for me to say what you can do on a bass in free jazz besides first yanking on the low E string, and then fiddling around on the higher ones before quickly attacking the low E string again. On the other hand, there was also the bow you could mistreat by vigorously scraping it backwards and forwards, brandishing it, forcing it to wrest tremolos from the strings, and scraping and scratching it some more until the bow hairs would gradually be torn out of their base. This playing around was costly because replacing all of the bow hairs every time you performed became unavoidable. But the art of this spectacle demanded sacrifices.

To my mind, whoever wants to be listened to has to respect certain rules, so that the ear can cope with what is being produced. Those who choose chaos as their one "true doctrine" run the risk of not being understood amid the confusion. This is as true of language as it is of music. Intermittent chaos is certainly justified – as a departure from the conventional, the normal. A melodious passage, suddenly interrupted, can be appealing. This type of tolerance is necessary. But it would be sheer nonsense to assume that unremitting turbulence can provide satisfaction in the long run. Faith in the "true doctrine" doesn't move mountains.

Today I have a clear position regarding free jazz:

I couldn't stand it.

I desperately wanted to take part in it.

I think free jazz is important.

This doesn't quite fit together? True. But what did back then? There was no way of breaking ranks without walking straight into a trap.

At least there were two separate camps. The hardcore advocates knew only one direction: going for it, no holds barred. Tone and time without meaning.

Along with Wolfgang Dauner, I belonged to the second direction: the "happening" faction, despised by the hardcore faction. No recognizable seriousness, derision suspected. This was the case at a notable concert in Frankfurt, a meeting of the German free jazz elite initiated and broadcast by Hessischer Rundfunk (HR).[1] I was there as one of the members of a special Dauner outfit: Wolfgang Dauner was the pianist (in theory), Jürgen Karg, the bass player, I, the cellist (oddly enough), Fred Braceful, the drummer (in theory) and Roland Wittich, the lighting technician (in actual fact, also a drummer). When the technicians of HR asked us where we would set up our instruments, all they received was unintelligible information: "Here, over there, kind of like this, uhm, and there, too!"

---

1. The public broadcasting corporation of the German federal state of Hesse.

This went on until the technical staff eventually had had enough of our antics and refused to record us. We weren't bothered in the least. Squares! Protest and upheaval were the order of the day!

A few words about our concept and its implementation: First, Dauner started plonking around on the piano. Then he operated a tape recorder that played a review of the work of Willis Conover, the American jazz pope of the time. Another programme, which presented the latest Dauner LP, suffered from severe fading: medium wave or short wave. The quality was poor. You could hear fragments of a review of the Wolfgang Dauner Trio – in English, of course. Fred Braceful and I were on at the same time as Wolfgang. Fred still had a combat uniform from his time in the army and wore it to carry me onstage in his arms. I held Mao's Little Red Book in one hand while lip-synching the Conover announcement. Inscrutable astonishment in the room. Faint tittering down below. Everything was more or less illuminated by Roland Wittich, who effected dramatic change with the use of occasional darkness. In the meantime, we hacked at our instruments, unheard, because the technicians hadn't set up any microphones – for a good reason.

The performance was supposed to end with a highlight. Fred Braceful intended to play the drums stark naked, fully aware that this would be seen as "inciting a public disturbance" and was punishable by law. Publicly exposing oneself – the police could have intervened. We wanted to avoid showing "too much," so we instructed our lighting technician to extinguish the light at the sound of a signal. It flickered most of the time anyway: nothing was supposed to be "normal." Roland Wittich was on the lighting bridge, but couldn't see the stage, which is why he needed the agreed-on acoustic signal. Chaos took its course, it became difficult to stay on top of things, confusion reigned – and there Fred was, naked onstage in the brightest of lights. Unusual for someone who wasn't an exhibitionist. He grabbed a bunch of drumsticks from his case and covered the most essential parts of his manhood until Roland eventually turned the lights off.

This put an end to our performance. It was met with enthusiastic applause. Had we been mistaken for a cabaret act? The acclaim couldn't have been on account of the music. That came later, played by the other faction, that of the "inquisitors." But our nonsense had undermined the seriousness of the evening. Representatives of the "true doctrine" reacted indignantly, dripping with contempt, accusing us of "trampling on their ideas."

Another free jazz event took place a bit later somewhere in the state of Saarland. Three "creators," all of them our age, were present. They told us about their compositions. The first had invented "semicircular conducting." One had to pay attention to when the maestro's arms closed or – the other way round – opened a semicircle. Only then could anything be altered in terms of sound. There were sample musical scores: one could play what was written, or radically change it. A further option was to play something completely different and just forget about the score. Absolute rubbish. This "conductor" would occasionally grab a pair of mallets in order to strike a strange vibraphone, producing even stranger sounds. I don't know how successful this creator of music became in later years.

Figure 13: The wild 1960s: Fred Braceful carries Eberhard Weber – holding Mao's Little Red Book – on to the stage

Karl Berger, originally from Heidelberg, was another very well-known vibraphonist at the time. He charmed us less with his musical notes than with verbal descriptions of how his compositions should be played. Attention please: each musician was to start off softly – with a note of their choice. This was first to be defined, then played around, then enriched by gradually adding other notes, etc. – "etc." really was an explicit part of his instructions. Eventually, we were supposed to all reach a grand climax together. Your attention one more time please: after exactly twenty minutes!

There must have been ten or twelve of us musicians. Players who aren't "free" cannot imagine how something like this goes down. After as little as about ten seconds, individual musicians began to engage in a guessing game: what else could we do with a single note? Ten seconds can be an eternity! Internal unrest arose: how were we to stretch this out to twenty minutes? And so, only ten seconds in, partial chaos erupted. A little thereafter, we cast secretive glances at our watches. Horror of horrors: "What? It's only been five minutes?"

The experienced hardcore player doesn't give up: he is familiar with the bludgeoning, and muddles on, ever louder, ever more frantic. Only now did I realize: no one could keep this up for twenty minutes, twenty minutes of mistreating one's instrument with all one's strength. This strength eventually runs out. And that is exactly what happened: we slackened. It might have been at the eighteenth or nineteenth minute. At the twentieth, Karl Berger checked his watch and noticed that no climax had been reached. The brilliant aim of his composition had not been met: "I'm sorry, we have to try again."

I have no idea how we managed to get through this rubbish again – presumably with the last shreds of our vigour.

The third "composer," Mani Neumeier, who later became the alt-rock band Guru Guru's drummer, blessed us with a drawing: three same-sized circles drawn in colour pencil, one red, one blue, one green. Mani had come up with a difficult task. All the contributors were divided into three groups. One followed the red circle, the other, the blue, and the third, the green. Each group could start and stop whenever they pleased. Yes, that's how it was.

Did it make any difference whether you listened to the "semicircular conducting," the "twenty-minute epos" or the "circular sound drawing"? Not the slightest bit! From start to finish, the three compositions sounded the same: chaotic din three times over.

I must confess that on one occasion my twenty-minute theory was challenged: a "free" trio from Japan consisting of a diminutive greenhorn on the alto saxophone, a similarly slight pianist and a wiry drummer kicked off with downright unimaginable energy. The racket was unremitting and incessant. I had to ask myself if the saxophone player ever took a breath. At this rate, it seemed obvious to me that after twenty minutes these physical exertions would have to end. If only! The three gentlemen steadily slogged on at the highest volume for thirty, forty, fifty minutes. No one took a single break, not even for a second. Finally, after an hour – I looked at my watch – they stopped. For no apparent reason. Musically, it did not follow. There was applause, most likely on account of their physical performance: if you only manage ten push-ups yourself, you will definitely be impressed by 250.

The three performers still didn't show any signs of fatigue. An encore ensued. This, too, lasted a solid half hour – and was in no way different from what had come before.

A story from my youth: one day the entire student body of my Gymnasium in Esslingen was asked to march to the local Church of Our Lady the next morning to partake of the Lord's Supper. Supper in the morning? So be it. I was already in my final year. Although the student movement of '68 was still in the distant future, a hint of upheaval was already perceptible. The pupils in my year may have agreed to march along in solidarity, but they refused "to take part in the circus at the altar!"

There was a glut of pupils at the time: three times more than usual in every school year. This meant that altogether around 800 pupils – three classes per year over nine years – gathered in the church: the first-years in front and the older pupils at the back. Then it started. One class after the next was summoned to the altar by their teacher so that each pupil, their tongue sticking out, would receive the host, the Body of Christ. His blood wasn't offered to us. Presumably, the parson had already siphoned it off for his supper.

As expected, everyone answered the call. Then it was the older pupils' turn. First, year seven, then year eight. Everything went according to plan. Among the pupils of year nine, I sat all the way in the back: we'd been asked to sit in alphabetical order. Weber – W was last. I got curious. No sign of solidarity yet. Everyone dutifully marched to the front – even after the year eight pupils were done. I had expected that a few pupils of year nine would get up and go to the front: in my class alone three were the sons of parsons. Breaking rank couldn't be expected of them. But when all my other classmates, so full of bravado the day before, started to follow the herd, I panicked. Even those I had complete confidence in rose from the pews – the most ardent leftists, the intellectuals, the class speaker. What were they doing? Only three more, only two more… Our teacher came over to me: "Weber, it's your turn!"

I clammed up, unable to say a word, and just shook my head. I was the only one of 800 pupils to remain seated. It was hell being left alone like that. I wasn't proud. Not at that point! But shortly thereafter, when we were led back to our classrooms and lessons started again, our teacher approached my bench. Was I going to be admonished? How was the only objector among 800 pupils going to be dealt with? "Hats off!" my teacher said softly.

My pride had been restored.

Years later, I asked myself if my breaking ranks at the time had marked the start of my musical otherness. Like so many others, I saw the student movement of '68 as a liberation from our parents' generation. All the same, I hit the brakes, wanting to avoid anything too impetuous. On one occasion, Wolfgang

Dauner had intended to slaughter a chicken onstage. Not on my watch! Was I square? Cowardly? Who knows? But to this day, I don't see any sense in slaughtering a chicken onstage. When did the slaughter of chickens become musical? The death cry of a chicken? At some point, it just gets distasteful.

I only ever had one private student. A fanatical free player, he wanted to learn to play the bass on a weekly basis. All he ever did – I swear it's true – is tug on his low E string. He wasn't capable of anything else. I met him again after a couple of months, at one of the legendary free jazz meetings in Baden-Baden. Wolfgang Dauner and I were invited, too. The whole thing still took place under the aegis of the "big chief," Joachim-Ernst Berendt, aka the jazz pope – or Joe, to us. He was the head of the editorial department dedicated to jazz at Southwest Broadcasting (SWF) Baden-Baden. Around twenty-five musicians were gathered at the SWF recording studio for a week. As I've mentioned before, there weren't any rules. We were ready to get started.

Who was to play with whom? Berendt knew who to ask: the saxophone player John Tchicai had to think of something. It didn't take him long. He said: "I'll take them all."

That meant twenty-five musicians all playing at once. To those who can remember these times: there rarely was much shilly-shallying. Things got going, and back then, that really meant: things got going! In no time at all, everyone was playing at full blast, giving it their all. Of the twenty-five musicians, all of them "damaged" by free jazz, only two played with instruments that weren't "thoroughbred": Wolfgang Dauner and I. Dauner blared into an admittedly ghastly wind device that failed to do much more than squawk electrically. I still had my original contrabass, which – dear me! – had been electrically amplified. Anyone who knows what they're doing will realize that with twenty-five guys blowing, beating and banging at full blast, details are inaudible. The human ear is overtaxed. It was also customary to play until natural exhaustion ensued. Based on experience, as mentioned earlier, this takes twenty minutes at most.

Now something odd happened. As the first signs of fatigue set in, it suddenly became possible to identify structures, to hear something. The other gentlemen became aware of the fact that something artificial was at play: Dauner's electric horn and my electrically powered contrabass. Appalled glances shot our way.

The only rule of the meeting was that everyone could play anything they wanted with anyone. Every "composer" called on by Berendt chose his own favourite musicians. Let me get back to my student, the one with the E string. As I said, he, too, had been invited. Apart from him, at least two other bass players were available, but "my" E string tugger was the busiest all week. Possibly this had to do with the fact that his unamplified contrabass remained effectively inaudible.

Dauner and I were idle for much of the week, witnessing the merciless din as mere spectators. After several days of abstruse recordings and monotony,

Berendt noticed that two people had been inactive ever since the initial twenty-five-musicians-at-once idea. Consequently, Wolfgang Dauner was now instructed to piece something together. After days of tonal chaos, Wolfgang asked me and the Swiss drummer Pierre Favre – we both knew him well – to form a trio.

We agreed on a spontaneous arrangement. We would determine how to fill a certain number of minutes in an engaging way without settling all the details. Wolfgang instantly had a concept at hand that was in keeping with his character: "Hey, we'll kick off full blast at full tilt."

After some time, I was supposed to play a few longer low notes that he would supplement with a few chords. Then more chaos.

At any rate, we had a concept. Time to record! The red light was on. Behind the window separating us from the control room, we could see most of the other musicians standing next to the producer, Berendt. Evidently, they were curious to see what we would deliver.

We kicked off full blast at full tilt. I hope you can forgive me for not explaining how one plays at "full tilt." Anyway, everything went well. Then came my slow low tones, accompanied by a few of Dauner's chords. Out of the corner of my eye, I could see a few of the musicians behind the pane of glass trying to persuade Berendt of something. Did they want to get rid of the balance between the piano, the bass and the drums? The red light was switched off. Berendt entered the studio, walked towards us, and, much to our surprise, addressed us in English: "This is a free jazz meeting. You can't play harmonies. It's not allowed!"

Free and verboten? The fact that he was revealing his true colours escaped him. This is what he was like, our super expert, *the* German authority on jazz.

We were shocked and baffled. We were neither able nor willing to present anything else, so we chose to present nothing. This was not accepted. We had been hired to take part in a free jazz festival! What else could we do? Out of necessity, we fell back on the usual solution: full blast at full tilt. We pounded away with our hands and feet, mistreated the keys, tore away at the low E string: "Fantastic! Thank you. Very good!"

Joe's favourite lead-in was: "No less a person than X said…" He had unrivalled knowledge of who had done what with whom, when and where. But he was a far cry from an expert when it came to his actual job, to music, or rather, musicality. Intonation problems or any other tonal details were beyond his depth. He was a producer. As such, he had lots of ideas about who could play with whom. But he could not assess tonal finesse. If things didn't quite work out, the "event" was hyped as an iconic idea, labelled "innovative," "progressive," "daring."

Oddly enough, Albert Mangelsdorff hadn't been invited to the unforgettable event in Baden-Baden. Neither had Peter Brötzmann, Manfred Schoof or Alexander von Schlippenbach – all most definitely candidates for experiments of this kind. Why Berendt chose this other, obscure combination instead remains a mystery.

To underpin this extremely odd choice of participants: another E string specialist wanted to play a solo according to the usual "scrape and scratch" principle. He asked for a piece of chalk, with which he drew a circle around him. Within this delineation, no microphones were allowed.

Yet another brilliant free jazz advocate decreed that his musicians had to play in the auditorium, between the tip-up seats, while the microphones remained in the studio. Everyone was impressed – including the German jazz pope, Joachim-Ernst Berendt.

To this day I ask myself why players of free jazz react physically as soon as they are in contact with an instrument. Their neck turns red and their arteries swell as if the instrument had to be wrestled to the ground. I have never seen a pianist, for example, start off with soft notes when they sit down at the keyboard. Careful, tender intuiting seems to be forbidden. Wind players instantly start with a sort of bellowing that is anything but soft. Admittedly I am no expert. I didn't keep up with the development of the hardcore faction after leaving it. But back "in my time," I don't remember there ever being a quiet part lasting longer than ten seconds. Free jazz calls for volume. As soon as ideology is involved, a switch is flipped in the thought process that forbids pulling out certain stops. Every form of jazz can be played softly and loudly, even brutally. Free jazz, on the other hand, obliges the players to permanently play at full throttle. Everything else is rejected as bourgeois, square and superficial. If you're not constantly forced into action, it isn't "free." If you want to change something about the establishment, it may well be necessary to resort to vehemence at times. I realize that. It's still a pity – you won't make yourself any clearer by just shouting. Here's a suggestion: perhaps the term "playing" should be forbidden, too: it implies playfulness, ergo, diversity, free play and lightness.

I am being polemical, I know. But I have always been a passionate observer – this has granted me many spectacular discoveries. And I enjoy talking about them – in full consciousness that they may be seen as defamatory.

In the course of my decades-long involvement in the scene, I have also witnessed plenty of situational comedy and humour besides the seriousness. Much of it is best left untold… Permit me just one little story about our jazz pope, Joachim-Ernst Berendt, aka Joe. We all knew that Joe was a pill freak. There was nothing he didn't use a pill for – or against. One day we were in Frankfurt's Centennial Hall. At the time, the coatroom and staffroom of the technicians and musicians were located under the stage, accessible via a narrow winding staircase. I was sitting downstairs with Albert Mangelsdorff when suddenly, in the middle of our conversation, we heard the door to the spiral staircase open above us, followed by the sound of countless pills bouncing down the stairs with no one in sight. Albert called out: "Joe, is that you?"

It was.

7 Telephone Bass Player

During recordings, the great German conductor Wilhelm Furtwängler still insisted on hanging just one microphone above the symphony orchestra, with at most one more above the audience in order to mix in the room acoustics. My interpretation is that Furtwängler believed that it was the music as a whole that mattered, more than the sound of any single instrument and its individual features. Consequently, he conducted the various groups of instruments according to their position relative to this one microphone: whoever sat directly beneath it had to be a bit more subdued; around the edges, more forcefulness was permitted.

In the maestro's defence, both microphones and recording technique as a whole were still in their infancy back then. In fairness, the sound I was able to experience as a child lying under a grand piano in a room full of musicians cannot be replicated live today, either. The grand piano is much too small for this and the audience, ideally, too large. It can also be assumed that the prospect of audience members attempting to lie under the grand piano would not fill the musicians with joy.

In the studio, however, things have moved on. Today, modern recording techniques make almost every effect possible. This started in the early 1960s. Back then, the idea of making individual instruments more audible was slowly taking shape. There's no denying that a violin sounds very different depending on whether you place it under your chin or listen to it from the last row. In old recordings, the grand piano was recorded with just a single microphone hanging above it. And for a long time the belief prevailed that what was right for classical music couldn't be wrong for jazz. However, slowly but surely, resistance and doubts began to grow. The goal now was to reproduce the sound of an instrument the way it is heard by the musician. Frequently, there were wars of opinions. What should an instrument sound like? Like in the room in which it is being played? I can hardly expect to sit in the musician's ear canal. I sat right next to a piano for decades and am still aware of the fact that it sounds completely different for the pianist – without even taking into account any kind of hearing impairment.

New ideas about sound emerged. What does it sound like if the microphone is placed inside the piano? Why only one microphone? Why not try three? One for the treble, one for the middle and one for the lower tones.

This brings me to MPS, an acronym for Musik Produktion Schwarzwald. At the beginning, the name SABA was still in use (wonderfully fusty: Schwarzwälder Apparate-Bau Anstalt).[1] They produced radios, telephones and television sets. SABA Records' studio was located on the company grounds. One of the two brothers who owned the company, Hans Georg Brunner-Schwer, known as HGBS, separated the label from the company in the late 1960s and founded MPS as a successor to SABA Records in 1968. It was the first German record label that exclusively dealt with jazz. Evidently, back then jazz was a genre that entrepreneurs still believed to be profitable. However, I doubt that this was HGBS's main motivation. The sale of SABA was rumoured to have earned him millions.

MPS was open to experiments even if it meant breaking character. I was lucky enough to get involved with HGBS very early on. I had become a telephone bass player, someone who was called up on the phone at short notice for studio recordings. MPS always had musicians "in transit" for new productions in the studio. Additional musicians had to be hired when necessary to turn a lone pianist or guitarist into a trio, for example. This is how I ended up playing with Art Van Damme, Hampton Hawes, Monty Alexander or the likes of Baden-Powell and Joe Pass. The latter was flown in from the States with the accordionist Art Van Damme, and, joined by another "telephone" colleague, we produced an Art Van Damme Quintet LP. Kenny Clare from the UK played the drums that time.

The executive producer was Willi Fruth, another old hand at MPS. During the recording he asked us if we wanted to record another LP as a trio. Knowing that we would be paid an additional fee for this, we immediately agreed. This is how *Intercontinental* came into being.

On top of these two LPs, Joe Pass was pushing Kenny and me to hurry so that we could record a third. The prospect of two extra fees was alluring! Unfortunately, our efforts were in vain. The producer didn't yield. But in spite of our haste, *Intercontinental* received very positive reviews.

This story is a very good argument against the idea that length of production equals quality. Who isn't familiar with reports praising pop band X, which "only" spent eight months in the studio to complete their latest CD! It never crosses the fans' minds that this might be proof of their idols' inefficiency. I have frequently had the opportunity to take part in pop productions and have often encountered an unwillingness to make decisions: "Let's record everything and decide later!"

---

1. Black Forest Machine-Building Institution.

Figure 14: At the MPS studio, Villingen-Schwenningen, July 1970

In jazz I was rarely faced with such deliberations. First of all, the number of tracks on a recording device was limited, so a decision as to what would be kept and what wouldn't had to be made. Financing shouldn't be forgotten, either. Jazz is not a mass product, so it really makes a difference how long the formations spend in the studio when every extra day costs a fortune. No wonder that jazz producers insist on timely decisions as to what should be recorded. At ECM the name of the game was: three days to wrap everything up (two to record, one to mix). Done. And it really worked. All my ECM LPs were produced following this procedure.

It is nerve-racking, though, especially if the recording didn't go so well on the first day – which happens quite often. Then everything has to get wrapped up on the second. Concentration has to be sustained, if necessary, all through the night.

I personally had this unpleasant experience when I recorded *Chorus* at Sound Studio Bauer in Ludwigsburg-Eglosheim with Jan Garbarek and Ralf Hübner. On the second day, things didn't go smoothly, either. The only solution was to use a small part of the third day, the mixing day, to finish recording. Unfortunately, our drummer had to be at another production in Frankfurt that day. As a result, he couldn't stay for the mixing. His train was scheduled to leave Stuttgart around 10 a.m. When we ran out of energy, around midnight on the second day, we decided to continue recording at six o'clock the next morning. Fully concentrated, we were due to finish two hours later, around eight. Then Ralf would pack up and rush to Stuttgart's central station to catch the ten o'clock train to Frankfurt.

Shortly after midnight we reached the hotel. As the one in charge, I now had to find a solution as to how we were going to manage the music. The problem wasn't our capacity to play, but my musical concept. I sat at the small table in my hotel room and thought about it. Lo and behold, there was a glimmer of hope: I wrote down the composition's new structure on a piece of paper. Off to bed now! Once I got there, thoughts kept floating around in my head. Up again to make corrections. Now it was just right. Back to bed. Why couldn't I sleep? Around two o'clock in the morning I was back at the desk: second correction. Finally, around three, I fell asleep. My alarm was set for five and the recording was due to start at six. I got up and raced to the studio without having breakfast. After warming up, quickly, we started recording.

Luckily, it worked out.

Back to the Black Forest, though: a few years before Manfred Eicher appeared on the market with ECM, it was Hans Georg Brunner-Schwer who stood for modern sound – and MPS was the only German label to deal with jazz.

Brunner-Schwer certainly didn't shy away from unconventional arrangements or anything unusual. Stereo had only just been installed and it was tempting to wallow in the new technical possibilities, put the ping-pong effect to use, and keep "left" and "right" as far apart as possible. HGBS took the bold step of moving Monty Alexander's very compact piano because it would have bothered another soloist during his solo: Ernest Ranglin, the Jamaican guitarist, was present at this session. After Monty's solo, Hans Georg moved the piano from the middle to the side, so that Ernest could play in the middle. Then he moved it back again. Presto! It feels strange when an instrument on the LP literally gets pushed aside.

I noticed early on that improvising in the studio involved a different set of challenges from the ones you encounter onstage. During an ECM production with Jan Garbarek in the Oslo studio – as was usual back then – I had a strange and interesting experience. For acoustic reasons some instruments are kept apart from others in the studio to avoid the sound of the drums, for example, getting picked up on the piano's microphone. In extreme cases, individual instruments are isolated in separate closed booths. This makes acoustic communication impossible – an unsurmountable challenge as far as improvisation is concerned.

The solution: headphones. The problem: the headphones' modulation. Each musician is allotted a tiny mixing desk with which the individual instrument can be mixed separately according to the musician's own preferences. So it's up to each and every one to choose the volume they deem appropriate for the recording. A really practical feature – or so I thought the first time I came face to face with it. Until I realized something which I considered alarming: each one of my colleagues, myself included, had turned up the volume of their own instrument to the max. One hundred percent, as it were. Yet we knew that hearing each other is just as important to create different harmonies. We knew that it is spontaneous mutability which, ideally, makes playing together so exciting.

We know that when the "harmonist," the pianist or guitarist, plays "their" harmonies, I, the bassist, can respond with one set of notes or another, thus "colouring" the harmonies. What happens, though, if no one listens to me, if my colleagues, as was the case in Oslo, don't realize that I am eliciting different harmonic possibilities? Cooperation becomes impossible when that happens.

In extreme cases, in the absence of a reaction from a colleague, it can happen that I play faultily or inappropriately. That's why on concert stages we always try to make sure the level control of the monitor speakers is properly calibrated: so that we can hear our colleagues play and communicate musically. Under certain circumstances, things can actually get more creative onstage than in the studio. In a "live" setting, it can even come to "exhibition bouts." Some people long for them. As far as Albert Mangelsdorff was concerned, the drums couldn't be loud enough. He would often nod in their direction encouragingly. Albert was a quiet, modest kind of guy; what he meant to say was: "Let them have it!"

A fine line separates doing it right from overdoing it. And as always: who decides which is which? And how do you do this in a music genre that values freedom so highly? During a rehearsal with Wolfgang Dauner and John Marshall at Stuttgart's Liederhalle, I had the opportunity to get told off by Chet Baker when he commented: "Aren't you a little loud?"

I can't help but feel a bit sorry if it was only through me that Baker learned that accompanists – not "co-players" (that's what this is really about) – believe that their contribution ought to be audible, and hope it will serve the (common) cause. But many soloists' principle is: me in front, you in the back. It seems to be in the nature of things that the melody always appears to be the most important thing. It was during a pop production of all things, with Kate Bush, that I realized that things can be quite different, that the arrangement can be given as much significance as the vocals. When this happens, an incredible density, a compactness, develops.

Never in sixty years have I ever heard a studio recording in which the bass was too loud. What I *have* heard are recordings in which the part played by the bass is so small that it is barely audible. What can we make of this? Has it never been recognized how important the bass is, how important low tones are for saturated musical sounds? What is so gruesome about low tones that they are only bearable when played in a subdued manner?

This early experience and the mistrust born from it led me to insist on always being present – to the extent it was possible – during the final mixing stage of studio productions. Without fail I asked for more bass every time. The same is true of the United Jazz + Rock Ensemble CDs I was involved in: absolutely everything is audible – every piano chord, all of the wind instruments, every part of the drums. And where are the bass notes even when the wind instruments are at it full throttle? Is everyone audible? It pains me when I take the trouble to find suitable notes and rhythms only to have the bass be degraded to a "boom-boom" accessory after the mixing. Although one does hear it somehow, it's classified as unimportant. In the obituary of a famous producer, the magazine *Der Spiegel* quoted the epitaph on his gravestone: "More bass, please." I can't remember this colleague's name. But I agree with him.

We musicians are now an endangered species. Who would have thought a few years ago that there would be chess computers capable of challenging world champions? Similarly, it has been possible for quite some time now to string together artificial sounds, note for note, from a violin, an oboe or a bass. During a symphony concert in front of a live audience, of course, a few irregularities can still crop up. If the recording is to be turned into a CD, one doesn't want to leave them in. What should be done? Repeat the concert in front of the audience? No, the audience has long left the hall. Instead, the orchestra gets called back onstage and the poorly executed parts are repeated and perfected without the audience present. An empty room sounds different from a full house? To remedy this, there is room acoustic equipment that simulates a full house. It gets inserted into the live recording. Perfect! No one notices the cheating. Even the soloist, the violinist or the pianist can intervene and make repairs. Hard to believe as it may be, the imperfections in a singer's intonation, too, can get "pitched" or bent into shape.

In short, no one is capable of telling apart what is real from what is artificial anymore. The term "artificial" has become superfluous; everything is "natural" somehow. Why should it be any different with music or recording techniques? We have long grown used to it in photography. Today, it is the camera, not the photographer, that is responsible for exposure or definition. Curse or blessing? Each one of us has to answer this question for themselves.

Over the decades, through the digitalization of studio technology, a development has taken place which de facto allows us to correct anything. With lightning speed. The old tapes have disappeared, and with them, the tediousness of cutting. The older ones among us are still familiar with desperate searches on studio floors: "Where has my prelude gone?" Gone are the MPS times when I was still a telephone bass player. Back then an ensemble with eight American musicians once held a public concert that MPS recorded for an LP. But, horror of horrors, it later turned out in the studio that the bass was barely audible on the recording, even after technical manipulations. The musician had long since departed. Once again, my phone rang. "We need you."

On the scene soon thereafter, I listened to the recording: nothing complicated, more like jazz routine. I recorded one track after the other, rarely having to play anything twice.

Only one spot proved to be tricky. My virtually inaudible colleague also played a prolonged solo! What was to be done? It was technically impossible to cut the solo. I couldn't play a satisfactory solo, either: of all places, right here the original bass kept coming through. After lengthy discussions, it turned out there was only one solution. I had to play as much and as fast as possible in order to "cover up" my colleague – even though I am not really known as a fast player. Still: no sooner said than done.

I would have loved to know what my colleague thought of this when he heard the recording much later on. Everything was under his name – I remained anonymous. Was he surprised by what his fingers had done during that concert?

I remained anonymous again when I received yet another phone call from MPS – this time I was needed for the bass part that was to be added to the solo recording of a Brazilian guitarist unknown to me. In a nutshell, I managed to keep the producer happy. But I was dissatisfied with the result. For this reason, I insisted on being mentioned on the cover only under a pseudonym. Producer Willi Fruth chose it for me: Juan Moreno. Olé!

8 "I'm gonna get myself one!"

It starts as it so often does. You want to talk about a film you saw with... uhm... that... hm... the one who... uhm... made the film with... at any rate... uhm... his partner was in the film...

I'd now like to talk about my cooperation with Volker Kriegel. It starts with our first meeting in the 1960s that never took place. In any case, we failed to meet back then in Düsseldorf when we could have met in the finals of the German Amateur Jazz Festival. We only realized this much later, when we did meet and got to know each other. It must have really started in Hamburg, then, when Volker supposedly met my future wife Maja, who was working in the jazz department of NDR.[1] It must have been a rather intense meeting. At any rate, it took place on the occasion of one of the well-known NDR jazz workshops. On a different occasion, Volker showed up there with his wife Ev, following which the two women became close friends. And so it could have happened that I met Volker on account of his wife's friendship with my wife-to-be.

At that point, our collaboration was still a long way off. Volker had minor band work in Frankfurt, I had some in the area around Stuttgart. Both of us were still rank amateurs. Participating in the German Amateur Jazz Festival required rehearsing. I had a guitar, bass and drum trio ready. Volker had the same idea. I'd picked a strange composition by the bass player Ray Brown that called for a somewhat complicated finger technique. The left hand has to press the notes on the fingerboard and pluck them at the same time. Not easy, but feasible – after all, Ray Brown was able to do it.

Volker, too, had chosen this piece. We entered the Schumann Hall in Düsseldorf with our two ensembles – each at a different point in time. While his bass player struggled with the Brownian technique, my guitarist wasn't up

---

1. Norddeutscher Rundfunk (Northern German Broadcasting).

to the level demanded by such a piece. Volker would have been a great addition to my trio, and I to his. Volker still swept the board.

He was awarded two prizes: one for best guitarist and one for best soloist. I don't want to nitpick, but it was astounding how many hair-raising wrong calls were made back then. Just because a pianist played quite decently and was awarded first prize, his bassist and guitar player were also chosen as best soloists. This so infuriated Wolfram Röhrig from South German Broadcasting, that he scheduled a concert in the Liederhalle's Mozart Hall to give another chance to those who really should have won.

It wasn't until years later that Volker and I discussed our Düsseldorf problems. Had we played together then, it's possible we would have won as a band and been flown to the USA to take part in a jazz festival as the opening act – only to be used as canon-fodder. This was quite common back then in the profit-oriented US, where an unknown European band wasn't worth anything, and would be put at the bottom of the bill.

Meanwhile, Volker and I still had to wait before we could meet. We ended up meeting… hm… it must have been when I… uhm … was it at Hessischer Rundfunk? Anyway, we met. From time to time, probably even with Albert Mangelsdorff. My friends have both died – who should I ask? How can I refresh my memory?

It must have been something like that. Thus began our casual cooperation. I continued to play as an amateur with Wolfgang Dauner in our duos and trios, and the jazz ensemble of Hessischer Rundfunk occasionally invited me to Frankfurt for a recording session on a Saturday morning even though I lived in Denkendorf, near Esslingen. Travel expenses were not an issue and an overnight stay wasn't necessary as I would always drive back immediately. The department responsible for travel expenses at HR occasionally even wired an allowance to cover the train journey to Deggendorf because in Frankfurt they would mix up Denken- and Deggendorf. I kept the higher fare; as a jazz musician, you had to look out for number one.

I must have met Volker Kriegel in the HR jazz ensemble – for a while he was a permanent member. Over time, I also started to be involved in recordings made in a private studio for commercials and television. Sometimes Albert would be the composer, at others it would be Volker, Joki Freund, Günter Kronberg or Heinz Sauer.

This reminds me of a highly embarrassing situation. Years earlier, Albert had recorded the title music for a culture programme on ARD[2] called "Titles, Theses, Temperaments."

One day, Volker Kriegel invited us into the studio. Albert was there, too. After the recording, he asked Volker: "What's the music for?"

---

2. Arbeitsgemeinschaft der öffentlich-rechtlichen Rundfunkanstalten der Bundesrepublik Deutschland (Working group of public broadcasters of the Federal Republic of Germany).

"The new opening titles for TTT."

The embarrassing thing was: neither of the two had realized that Albert had just helped carry his own title music to the grave.

Since these recording sessions were often quite long, I occasionally brought Maja, now my wife, along. We would spend the night at the Kriegels' in Wiesbaden. This is how our friendship developed.

Maja and I had met on 18 November 1967 in Hamburg. I was playing at a concert with the Wolfgang Dauner Trio that day. Since she was working in the jazz department of NDR, she had been commandeered to look after the artists. Afterwards we arranged to meet at the Hamburg Jazz House for a drink. Was it love at first sight? At the very least, we were both dazed and confused by what was going on with us, or rather, that something was going on. But after hours of intense conversation, of all people, Maja kissed Wolfgang goodbye. Not me.

On the train ride back to Stuttgart, I was in a state of unrest. I was resolutely determined to send a bouquet of flowers to her department the next day – I didn't have her home address. So I did, with Fleurop. That evening, as usual, I dropped by my parents' place. As I entered the flat, I heard my mother say: "Just a moment, here he comes!"

It was Maja! "Dazed" herself, she had looked for my address at work and only found that of my parents.

The abridged version: eight months later, we got married in Esslingen am Neckar on 28 June 1968. Why so soon? For professional reasons we could only meet at weekends. Sometimes I would drive to Hamburg, at others she would fly to Stuttgart. This cost money. Prosperity was a long way off. As a "double earner," I had to help out with the airfare from time to time. After ten exciting weekends, we decided to end the to-ing and fro-ing and seek a legal union – in the frantic years following the student movement of '68, landlords were panicking. More and more flat-sharing communities were being founded and unmarried couples wanted to move in together. This, however, wasn't so simple. The notorious procuration paragraph was still in effect. Whoever "procured," tolerated or granted the opportunity to facilitate illicit sexual relations (including sexual relations out of wedlock) was punishable with no less than one month in prison. We had to get married. Not because offspring was on the way, but because we needed a flat.

White for the bride and black for the groom wasn't really our thing. In this respect, we were true to the student movement of '68. On leaving the registrar's office, Maja and I even thought about getting divorced. For one thing, we had found a flat in the meantime, and for another we realized on signing the marriage certificate that we had just tied ourselves to each other contractually for life. We had just given up our beloved freedom.

For my father, our non-traditional wedding must have been the end of the world. He missed the indispensable ceremonies. But the times of "dressing smartly" were over. In one of its issues, *Der Spiegel* wrote: "Corduroy trousers and longer hair are hallmarks of the enemy." This was true in many respects. Taxis mercilessly drove past us when they saw our kind trying to hail them.

Figure 15: Maja Weber, 1970

Years later, I discovered that my father had secretly had wedding cards printed and mailed them to his relatives. What did they say? The usual folde-rol: "Dr Hans Weber and wife Hildegard have the honour of announcing the wedding of their son to the daughter of ... etc."

Figure 16: Eberhard and Maja Weber on 28 June 1968 at the Esslingen registrar's office

A bank account had to be opened. This brought about an especially telling scene. A form was being filled out by an employee based on our responses to his questions. I was registered as a musician. Maja answered truthfully his question as to what occupation she was in: "None!" That was the case at that moment; she had left her job at NDR. So the bank clerk wrote: "Housewife." Women's emancipation still had a long way to go.

Through Maja, I came to know a very different conversational culture. In Hamburg, in my wife's home, a spade was called a spade. Everything was discussed, and if necessary, argued about openly. In the Webers' home, on the other hand, anything unpleasant had always been swept under the car-pet. There wasn't much room left under the carpets of my parents' home. Right after our wedding, I had the chance to experience Maja's open nature personally. My first gift to her, a red handbag, was instantly used to upbraid me. Did I really not know her any better than this? But how can you know someone after just ten weeks? On one occasion, we went through the absurd experience of not finding each other in a department store after losing sight of each other. What does Maja look like from behind in a crowd? I don't know what her clothes look like yet! She experienced something similar. We only became familiar with each other's idiosyncrasies later. We lived in

Esslingen-Wäldenbronn, in a small modern penthouse on Talstrasse, and later on in Denkendorf, near the Filder, a slightly undulating, fertile plateau.

This was the time when we regularly visited the two Kriegels in Wiesbaden as by now our collaboration in the Dave Pike Set had begun. The American vibraphonist had been playing with Volker in a quartet for a while, and they had been busy touring with the Austrian bass player Hans Rettenbacher and the Frankfurter drummer Peter Baumeister. Over a period of four years, they had done pretty much everything there was to do: they were very successful. However, little by little, constantly being on tour started taking its toll, and one day, when Hans Rettenbacher couldn't make it, I was invited. We played a gig together, and I made every effort to make a good impression. As had happened years before with the Dauner Trio, I became a member of the New Dave Pike Set practically overnight, having to tell Wolfgang Dauner that a different band now took precedence as far as I was concerned. He swallowed hard – after all, we'd been together for about ten years – and seemed to accept my offer to keep working with him whenever possible. His frustration lasted no more than a night. Then the telephone rang: "Hey, I think it's better we go our separate ways now."

By this time, I had landed in IBM's advertising department in Sindelfingen, and was getting paid quite handsomely for corporate films and commercials. As my wife gradually became aware of how unhappy I was there, she encouraged me to hand in my notice as soon as possible to finally do what I really had a gift for: making music.

"Let's just jump in at the deep end. We'll either float or go under."

No sooner said than done. To the astonishment of my bosses at IBM, I left my well-paid job in advertising after only half a year – and learned to swim with the New Dave Pike Set with good prospects of success in the not-too-distant future. The job at IBM had satisfied the need for security I was brought up with. And now, for the free life of a musician! The drummer of the Dave Pike Set, Peter Baumeister, had done the exact opposite on realizing that a job at a bank would be significantly more lucrative. It helped that his father owned a credit bank: he joined it, later taking over the financial institution.

So, Volker, Dave and I looked for a new drummer. Tony Inzalaco had just left the Kurt Edelhagen Band and was on the lookout for something new. We arranged an audition, and found that although Inzalaco was an outstanding drummer, he had too much of a big-band feel for our purposes. Dave, the band leader, should have been the one to convey the declination, but he tasked Volker and me to tell Tony that we were looking for more of a combo drummer. We did so heavy-heartedly. Tony thereupon complained bitterly to Dave, who wiggled out of it by saying that "in principle" he would have wanted him. It was I, then, who had to bear the brunt of his tirade. He was fuming. "I'd rather play with a one-armed bassist than with Eberhard Weber!"

Today, he could have the two rolled into one... During a chance encounter years later in a New York jazz club, we couldn't help but laugh at this old story.

Dave, Volker and I eventually found a very alternative young Swiss drummer called Marc Hellman – and travelled to Brazil. We had a benefactor there, Roland Schaffner, the head of the Goethe Institute in Salvador (Bahia). He succeeded in getting the Goethe Institute to invite us on a short tour of Brazil, all expenses paid, and rented an old villa near the beach where we wanted to prepare for a record – with three Brazilian percussionists. Thanks to them, I can now tell you about the longest time I have ever had to wait for a rehearsal. We had agreed to start at ten in the morning. A housekeeper made breakfast. Then we waited. Around one o'clock the good soul served us lunch: "Where are your three guests?" We would have loved to know. Around seven, just before dinner, the first of our three colleagues arrived: "I'm the first? There was no need to hurry, then!"

After that, things happened at lightning speed. By ten o'clock the last of the three percussionists had arrived. Twelve hours later than planned, or twelve hours late in European terms, we were able to begin. We rehearsed in our inner courtyard until long after midnight. Neighbours perched on the walls surrounding it, listening closely. In our part of the world, this sort of thing was unthinkable after midnight. In Frankfurt, during the "Concerts in the Palm Garden" series, the police were called immediately if complete silence didn't reign by ten o'clock. It was always incredibly difficult to give the audience an encore under those circumstances. The only solution: finish at nine forty-five, then add about ten minutes for the "extras." Sometimes, we would already hear the wailing sirens of approaching police cars during the encores.

Yet in Europe, too, I have witnessed more relaxed atmospheres – in Madrid, for example. During an open-air concert in the middle of the city-centre, neighbours and local residents settled on cushions at their windows and listened peacefully until long after midnight – without anyone calling the police.

I have to admit that when it comes to punctuality, I have remained very Swabian. To this day, I don't see what is supposed to be so exciting about waiting. The consequences of my stroke have caused me to be even more critical of tardiness because from the agreed-on time, I remain stuck, "walled up in the earth so steady,"[3] unable to allow myself a little detour to put to use the time spent waiting. Everything takes much longer than it used to. I can't help but see tardiness as insolence, as a sheer lack of consideration.

I have good friends whose first sentence on arriving is: "Sorry we're late!" What does one say to that? Just smile? Every time?

"It's not a big deal. These things can happen."

But let's get back to the New Dave Pike Set. As is so often the case with rehash – the band never really took off. And so, after a depressing performance at a billiard club in Esslingen, we decided to end things. I can clearly

---

3. "*Festgemauert in der Erden*," from Friedrich Schiller's poem, "The Song of the Bell." C. Huth, M. Wertz and R. Kokinda, *Friedrich Schiller: Poet of Freedom, Vol. II*, translated by Marianna Wertz (Washington, DC: Schiller Institute, Inc., 1988).

remember this last performance: it was depressing. There was hardly anyone in the audience. We had to spread out our amps and speakers on billiard tables, still trying – chin up! – to manage a decent finale. It was brutal having to end things so miserably. For the Dave Pike Set, this was the definitive end of an extremely successful time. And for Volker and me? We knew we would carry on together.

On account of my close collaboration with Volker and the great friendship between Maja and Ev, we Webers had moved to Wiesbaden as early as 1971, into an attractive old apartment building on Niederwaldstrasse, right around the corner from the Kriegels' home in a gorgeous, equally old residential building typical of the city's architecture.

Then all the discussions that usually take place when a new band is formed began: What should we call it? Who would we bring in? Who was going to be the leader?

Volker took over the lead, partly because we were going to stay under the same management as the Dave Pike Set had been. And he already had a clear idea of the direction in which he wanted to take the band: jazz rock. I wanted to make my own contribution, a good mix of jazz and rock.

It was clear to us both that we would have to find a piano with a synthesizer, and drums. Who came into question? Who was available? The electric piano, the famous Fender Rhodes, had burst onto the global scene, and the first serviceable specimens of the synthesizer appeared on the market. We envisioned wondrous sounds and rhythms. So, who played the piano well and had any experience with these new types of sound? Volker mentioned Jasper van't Hof from the Netherlands. He was just starting to make a name for himself, occasionally appearing in Germany with various bands. I was all for it, holding Jasper in high regard. But as these things go, suddenly a new name popped up. Much good was being said about this pianist. Hitherto unknown to me, I had heard him play with Eiliff, a band I was equally unfamiliar with. I thought: "This pianist is worth listening to more closely."

It was Rainer Brüninghaus. I must have felt that there was something unusual about him. I didn't want to lose sight of him, so I recommended him to Volker. We played a trial concert with each of the accused, but that didn't bring us any closer to making a decision. Both were excellent, both had a great feel for new sounds. Ultimately, we went with Brüninghaus. The decisive factor was that Rainer could read music perfectly. At the time, Jasper still had a tenuous grasp on this. As a professional, you don't feel like waiting until colleague X is ready, too. Even if you clearly sense great talent.

Next, the drums: who came into question? From my time working with Dauner, I knew there was a shortage of drummers in Germany. On a few, rare occasions, I had been asked to join the Michael Naura Quartet, with Joe Nay on the drums. Since Naura's quartet only played very rarely, Joe would be available. He turned out to be the biggest car freak. Without the slightest shred of evidence, he would repeat over and over again that he had been a test driver for Maserati – sometimes it was Lamborghini. On a regular basis, he would think about going back to his old job. On the rare occasions one of these vehicles happened to drive past us, his eyes would become transfixed, and he would invariably say in his Berlin dialect: "I'm gonna get myself one."[4] Aware of his chronic lack of money back then, we were unable to suppress a grin. His mantra became our dictum. Be it in a canteen, when someone got up to get a cup of coffee, or on countless other occasions, for a while, Joe's slogan always seemed to fit: "I'm gonna get myself one." In a bitter twist of fate, years later, Joe died from the injuries he sustained in a car crash. Heading home one night, he sped into an obstacle just before reaching his destination. According to the police report, there were no skid marks. He'd been driving neither a Maserati nor a Lamborghini.

But back to the year 1973: our quartet was complete! It being the early 1970s, we were of the opinion that equality was indispensable. This was totally different from the situation in the States. Dave Bargeron, who played with Blood, Sweat & Tears, the American jazz rock band that had just shot to fame, told me once that it was customary on the other side of the pond for fees to vary wildly.

We preferred the European model, where everyone receives equal payment. The names on the posters are all written in the same colour, in equally big letters. Everyone is equal. Although Volker and I tried to apply this principle at all times, we encountered stiff resistance from the media. After quite a few glasses of wine and beer, we finally settled on a name for our band: Spectrum. But after our very first tour, the media torpedoed it. The reviews, though positive, did not mention Spectrum – instead, they mentioned Volker Kriegel's Spectrum. The rest of us considered this an impertinence. But there was nothing we could do. Once the name caught on, it proved impossible to change. Later on, I went through the same thing with my band Colours. The media turned it into Eberhard Weber's Colours. That's the way it goes in the business. As if it wasn't hard enough to put together a programme that works, to top it off, you had to assuage your bandmates every time the "boss" got all the attention – something that shouldn't have happened in the first place, had the initial plans been respected by the press.

Spectrum rapidly became successful, touring regularly, and released the LP *Mild Maniac* with MPS – despite this, the formation didn't stay together long. Volker wanted to move further and further in the direction of jazz rock, which also meant endlessly rehearsing individual phrases to make them ever more precise and crisper. This was too fixed for my taste. I dreamed of something more open, more malleable. Rainer was on my side. Over the course of many nights, Volker and I discussed our differing approaches – contentiously, but without arguing. After all, we'd been the closest of friends and neighbours

---

4. *"Den hol ick mir."*

for years. Eventually, I couldn't help but form my own band. Volker carried on with younger musicians, from 1975 as the Mild Maniac Orchestra.

Maja and I remained lifelong friends with Volker and Ev. We took turns visiting each other regularly, and every time Volker sent us one of his caricatures, Maja would frame it and hang it on our wall immediately – it made our flat look very special.

Figure 17: Self-caricature by Ev Kriegel from the 1980s or 1990s

Over the years, Maja turned our flat into a private exhibition of Volker's and – increasingly – her own artwork. Having left the NDR jazz department and finding herself "demoted" to the position of housewife, she had discovered her love of painting. Initially, she just doodled around a bit, trying out colour pencils and water colours. First one thing, then another. Occasionally, she would ask me for help if she had trouble with things like perspective. Her first work of art was a joint effort. She was responsible for the artistic, I for the technical side. Under these circumstances, a piece was created, which, although spontaneously conceived, was still a far cry from Maja's later style. The term "naïve" was still wholly justified at this point. The piece was bursting with colour. The only word to come close to describing it was "colourful." Nonetheless, the guitarist Peter Horton asked her if he could use it for the cover of one of his LPs. And so a burgeoning career creating cover art began for Maja.

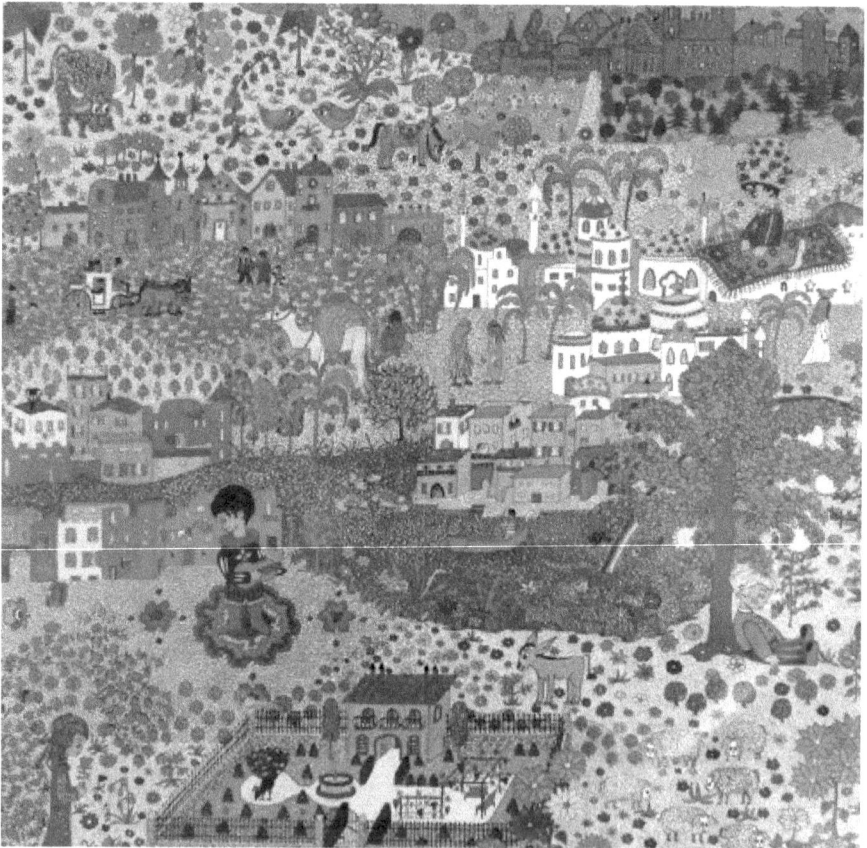

Figure 18: Maja's "firstling," which Eberhard Weber also contributed to, dated 1969

I, too, asked to use Maja's ever more distinctive and stylistically confident work for my ECM LPs. Over the years, her initially naïve, amateur technique evolved into a sort of "professional naivety." Maja designed the covers for all my ECM records. We would choose them together, often being of two minds. Having painstakingly reached an agreement and presented it to Manfred Eicher, the ECM producer, it still could happen that we would have to start all over. It's not easy to get artists to agree with each other. At ECM, she also provided the cover art for Steve Kuhn, John Abercrombie and Bill Frisell.

Maja also had an admirer of her artwork in Japan, and regularly received commissions from him. Volker and I were jealous. The Japanese market, in particular, was not easy for us. At regular intervals, we would compete as to who had sold the fewest copies in the Far East. At times it was five, at others only three. A strikingly different type of pride!

Figure 19: Eberhard Weber, drawn by Russell Hall, around 2008

Maja and I were often faced with the question of whether to sell her pieces – there was a lot of interest. I was the one to stop her – for very selfish reasons. I didn't want any bare walls at home. Maja was a very slow drawer and often took months to finish a single piece to her satisfaction.

Sadly, there are no new drawings from Volker or paintings from Maja. Fate decided otherwise. Volker died of a heart attack in 2003 after a long battle with cancer. And after Maja's sudden death in 2011, the typical, highly acclaimed ECM graphics were used for my last CDs. Some fans regret this. I miss having new pieces from Maja. And much more.

I have turned into a "normal" ECM musician. My covers all march to the same tune now. But at home, visitors still linger in front of the walls, moving from one drawing to the next, from painting to painting to see who is depicted with whom, and figure out how to interpret this or that caricature.

9 New Colours

Maja started taking care of my career early on. Part of the deal was her exhortation not to remain a sideman my whole life, to compose, to go my own way. Fine and dandy. Easier said than done – I didn't know how to compose. Although I could read music and chord symbols, I was mostly unsure of what exactly they meant. To get ahead and learn how to actually compose, I intended to ask a pianist friend about the meaning of something like Bb7, for example. In the end, I didn't want to expose any weakness, so I sat down and started analysing chord symbols, independently studying composition. After all, Arnold Schönberg wrote the epochal *Theory of Harmony* without ever having studied composition. How hard could it be?

Well, it wasn't easy. First of all, I had to find out how I was going to compose. Like a great classical composer at a high desk? No way! I had to hear what it sounded like. To that end, I needed an instrument. The bass? Too one-dimensional. Mine might have been marginally suited for melodies, but the piano proved easiest for me. Too bad I didn't know how to play it. So I had to slowly learn, which led to the strange phenomenon that, as a non-pianist, all I was ever able to play was the piece I was currently working on. As soon as I started a new composition, I had to start learning to play the piano all over again. Everything I'd learned to play previously just vanished into thin air. All these years, I only ever composed on the piano. There was one exception: the classical guitar. My fingering was even more limited on the latter. The result? *Yellow Fields.*

I set up a small studio in Wiesbaden with an electric piano, a tape recorder and a microphone. Everything was very rudimentary, plain and unassuming back then. I still made good progress because I was able to hold on to my initial naivety, and I wasn't afraid of trying out something new or unfamiliar. The offshoot of the student movement protected me: you could make music with anything. I used the piano stool as a replacement for the bass drum. I used my fist to hit the stool, on which I had placed the microphone – I liked this new bass drum sound! I started making up my first few pieces, and wrote them down on music paper in pencil, a far cry from today's computer-assisted composing. Bear in mind that the equipment of the 1970s was far removed from the quality of today's equipment and the possibilities it offers. I had one of the legendary Braun tape recorders from the time when Braun was still raking in design awards. They looked great, but didn't compare with today's technology. The word "digital" was literally an alien concept. But you cut your coat according to your cloth, and the results were actually quite astounding. Sometimes, I would present different versions to Spectrum. On one occasion, it was a song using a fifteen-beat rhythm, with bars consisting of fifteen quarter notes. You can hear it on my first LP *The Colours of Chloë*. It's not easy to play if you're used to a time signature of 4/4. Odd time signatures are not favoured in the West. In this part of the world, we have been "damaged" by 3/4 and 4/4 time signatures, accustomed as we are to perceive everything in blocks of three or four. So how does one play 15/4? Ideally, by breaking it down: 4/4 three times and 3/4 once equals 15/4. Too bad, that we're so used to perceiving in set blocks. This causes us to perceive 3/4 more like 4/4, so that the result is four times 4/4, which equals 16/4. Over time, I got so used to the odd fifteen-beat rhythm, that when my colleagues and I recorded completely different 4/4 pieces, I always finished before them: I would simply leave out one quarter. This drove the Swabian recording engineer to pose a question more commonly asked by Baden-Württemberg's innkeepers: "Can I get you another quarter?"[1] It took a while until I got the joke.

While I love complex rhythms, I probably love complex chords even more. For my last recording of *Résumé*, I drove back to the studio – one and a half hours away – just to counterbalance a final chord: I was missing the note that would "upset" the normal sequence the most. These "upsets" give me goose-bumps, instantly attracting my attention. This somewhat different form of harmonic obsessiveness means that certain very popular styles of music with simple harmonies are simply out of the question for me. Time and time again, it pains me how thoughtlessly the banal is often favoured. Not just in terms of harmony: why do fans of a particular band – whose recordings they all possess – spend good money on concert tickets if they aren't going to listen? Instead, they spend the entire time singing along and clapping, ideally in time to the music. No one can make me believe that it's possible to listen to music while jumping about or waving a lighter during slower pieces. I, for my part, go to concerts to listen, and to restaurants to eat. Would I ever be expected to sway a candlestick for the chef? As far as I know, for the time being at least, none of this nonsense has infiltrated jazz.

When I see how little real music education most German children are given in their first years of life, I am not surprised by this development. The

1. *"Derf ich Ihne no a Viertele brenga?"* In Swabian, a "quarter" refers to 0.25 litres of wine.

"distorted" music of the East with its trademark quarter tones remains a closed book in the land of the *Well-Tempered Clavier*, where it is considered "impure." South America – specifically Brazil, with its tricky syncopation and harmonies – is equally excluded from our "pat-a-cake, pat-a-cake" musical education. This is most likely due to the fact that only a few teachers have learned these musical structures and understand them. Which, in turn, is due to the fact that their teachers didn't understand them. Because, in turn… *perpetuum mobile.*[2] Miseducated this way, how can one not fall prey to the mass hypnosis of the rock and pop industries? My dear colleague Charlie Mariano used irony to answer the question of whether he liked one pop band or another: "I like their harmonies, both of them."

How can an audience that was never given any choices in early childhood make musical choices later in life? Does it lead to enlightenment when babies have heavy metal blasted at them because their parents don't know any better, convinced they are teaching their offspring what proper music is? In doing so, they merely steer their children towards a music industry that rejoices in the plainness and malleability of its listeners.

I have no children of my own, which, if you believe what many parents say, gives me no right to contemplate children's wellbeing. In the early days, when Wolfgang Dauner and I, as his accompanist, used to play for the SDR children's TV programmes, it always ended up sounding like Dixieland. This would indicate that music for children is supposed to be as simple and insignificant as possible. What a tragedy! Surely it is the scat singing found in jazz that most closely resembles children's utterances and what they are familiar with: *laba, bla ba du bi duah.* Many parents and grandparents even imitate their little ones in this way – without ever thinking of jazz. I imagine there aren't too many parents or legal guardians as absurdly talented as Ella Fitzgerald or Bobby McFerrin. Brazilian babies most certainly aren't born with greater capacities than babies in Europe, yet later in life, they are able to follow rhythms that baffle the rest of us. Allowing jazz in the cradle might be a way of broadening musical horizons later on. Children's music doesn't have to be simple.

With all due respect to harmonic and rhythmic complexity: I want to remain intelligible, musically as well as linguistically. As a listener, I can't stand it when I get the feeling that I am not taken seriously, when someone gives clever speeches, but leaves the audience in the dark. I don't like being left in the dark. Even my most jarring, craziest sounds should be intelligible, although I have always kept the artistic freedom to decide why I choose a particular means.

---

2. "Perpetual motion" here describes a musical composition that has the same rapid motion from start to finish.

Figure 20: Eberhard Weber around 1972

And so, with my originally naïve technical equipment, I began working on my very first LP, piece for piece, slowly but steadily. *The Colours of Chloë* was made in Wiesbaden. Initially, I had offered MPS the production, but they seemed to value me more as a telephone bass player than as an artist in my own right – my offer was rejected.

When I contacted ECM shortly thereafter, I was immediately invited to Munich. I had met the founder and head of ECM, Manfred Eicher, many years before, at the dawn of the free jazz era, on a stage, where he and his future partner, Thomas Stöwsand, were bustling around with instruments. Eicher was swinging little bells of some sort while Stöwsand was forcing sounds out of his bassoon. The two of them hardly managed more than chaos. Still, everyone was on the lookout in an atmosphere of emergence and upheaval, and so was Manfred Eicher, who had started out as a classical contrabass player.

Then, one day, Eicher started a record company. ECM was founded in 1969, quickly earning a reputation for being a kind of countermovement to free jazz: "The most beautiful sound next to silence." Wow! Gradually, word got around that forms of sound that were still being categorically rejected by other record companies were actually possible in Manfred Eicher's. Hurrah! Softer sounds and beauty were allowed again.

Around the time ECM was founded, I played a concert in Munich at Circus Krone with the Wolfgang Dauner Trio. I only found out much later, that Jan Garbarek had listened to our concert with Manfred Eicher. Jan was in Munich back then to discuss a production with Manfred. Eicher had started surrounding himself with Scandinavian musicians early on. In the process, he had discovered his favourite studio in Oslo with the sound engineer Jan Erik Kongshaug. Garbarek suggested to Eicher: "You ought to do a production with the bass player at some point. He seems interesting to me."

I was completely unaware of this encounter when, years later, armed with my tape recorder, I appeared in the smallest office in the world, on the first floor of the Elektro-Egger building in a part of Munich called Pasing. The office was barely big enough for a small desk and the boss's chair. The two chairs for Maja and me had to be squeezed in somehow. Everything went according to plan, my various excerpts and proposals were met with approval, and an appointment was made for a recording session at Sound Studio Bauer in Ludwigsburg-Eglosheim. This endeavour was a gamble for ECM as much as for me. Firstly, because all I had to show for were the experiments that I'd carried out at home on my tape recorder – it was my very first production. Secondly, because my ideas didn't really fit into any existing categories; I wanted to venture into uncharted territory, in matters of composition as much as any other.

Figure 21: Eberhard Weber and Manfred Eicher in the studio, 1972

Delighted with Eicher's positive answer, Maja and I drove back home and waited for the appointment at the recording studio. I prepared as well as I could. To this day, my ideas can be seen scrawled on the "score". In theory. In reality, I can't really make out what I wrote anymore. I had to rely on hieroglyphs as I wasn't familiar with some of the standard notations yet. At least back then I was able to decipher and explain them to those who had to perform them. Besides Rainer Brüninghaus on the piano and synthesizer, I decided to have Ack van Rooyen perform a solo on the flugelhorn. In addition, I wanted Paul Motian, the American drummer, to join us because one of the compositions was to be called 'No Motion Picture.' A great gag, I thought, if Paul *Motian* were among us. But it came to nought – Motian wasn't available. So I asked Peter Giger, from Switzerland.

We were all set to get started. I had rather unusual technical ideas that could be implemented instantly these days, but required a lot of tricks back in 1972. I had discovered shutter options on my Braun tape recorder, and now wanted to use this slight delay, which caused a distinct, comical rhythm. Would it be possible with the professional equipment in the studio? It wasn't easy, but the personal pride of the two technicians made it happen.

Of all the tracks on the LP, it was the eponymous 'Colours of Chloë' that simply wouldn't work out in the studio. My composition was too rudimentary, too unfinished. All of my tinkering was futile; we couldn't finish the LP. The only solution was to go home again and come up with a better solution. It took a few months until I was ready. By the time the second recording session started, I had come up with the song's striking melody. The problem was that now Peter Giger wasn't available anymore. Luckily, in the jazz ensemble of Hessischer Rundfunk I had met and learned to appreciate Ralf Hübner, Alfred Mangelsdorff's drummer. This is how he came to be the drummer on the title track, 'The Colours of Chloë.'

I owe the title of the song and the LP to Maja. She'd been using a box of colour pencils with the inscription "40 Colours." And while I was still in my tiny home studio, trying to record various tone colours on my Braun tape recorder, first one way, then another, I also used a little flute, an ocarina. Evidently, I kept repeating two notes, that somehow sounded like "O – E." Until Maja came over and said: "'O – E' – that sounds like 'Chloë.'"

"Colours" and "Chloë" added up to *The Colours of Chloë*. It was that easy, that simple. Incidentally, the name Chloë comes from Maurice Ravel's suite *Daphnis et Chloé*. No hidden mysticism of any kind here, I'm afraid.

Nevertheless, the naming of a composition is an interesting matter. Sometimes I agonized over titles for years, trying ever so hard to find something that wouldn't immediately be confused with a pre-existing piece. Luckily, my wife helped me with this. She was the one to find most of the titles, flipping through English-language books – *Winnie-the-Pooh* comes to mind. A few titles are my own creations: *T. On A White Horse* had to do with Pat Metheny's girlfriend at the time. She was Thai, and as her given name seemed too difficult to pronounce, she went by "T." *An Evening with Vincent Van Ritz* was created with Spectrum on a small island in Brazil when we were sitting in an unpretentious beach restaurant with little thatched "oases." We kept ordering tiny smoked fish. All around us, stray dogs lolled about, waiting for scraps. One of them had only one ear. It slowly starts to make sense: we called the restaurant Ritz, and gave the one-eared dog Van Gogh's first name. And since it was getting dark: *An Evening with Vincent Van Ritz*. I am also responsible for boring titles, such as *Chorus I – VII*. Later yet, on *Résumé* and *Encore*, I was able to simply name the pieces after the cities they were recorded in. This saved me having to think about titles too much.

Before the release of *The Colours of Chloë*, a guessing game unfolded as to how the music could be classified. Somehow or other, I had created great music that people liked, but it was not "real" jazz. The American market reacted surprised: here was something from Europe – which drawer did it belong in? Not even Manfred Eicher knew how to label the music, so he asked me to write an accompanying press release, which I did. Years later, I still noticed the words and descriptions I had chosen pop up in reviews even though quite a few things had changed by then.

One day, Eicher called me: "*Chloë*'s won the Great German Record Prize[3] and you've been named Artist of the Year 1975."

I hadn't even realized that my LP was in the running, so I was thrilled – all the more so because I was the winner of a category encompassing all music genres, including German *Schlager* and pop. This caused a stir in the industry. What was a jazz musician doing here, and winning on top of that, putting popular singers like Udo Jürgens in their place? Immediately, new categories were devised and introduced for the following years, so that there could be more winners – I'd fought quite honourably in 1975 because there was a lot more competition then than in the years that followed.

There was no prize money, just a certificate and a little plastic column that I couldn't even accept in person as I had an urgent job to do that day. The rent had to be paid.

After that, I headed back south. As I was no longer playing with Spectrum, there wasn't much point in living in Wiesbaden anymore. Now I wanted to be closer to ECM, so Maja and I moved to Bavaria. We found a little house to rent in Gröbenzell, near Munich, in 1976. Prompted by the experience I'd gathered by then, and my budding success, I installed a little home studio there, as in all of our future apartments, as well. A new LP was made in each of my home studios. On average, we moved every two to three years, so every two to three years, I recorded a new record.

---

3. *Großer Deutscher Schallplattenpreis.*

Figure 22: A housewarming party at the Webers'

We had a housewarming party in Gröbenzell, and as chance would have it, several of my colleagues were in the area at the time: Jan Garbarek with his Scandinavian quartet, and Ralph Towner, on tour as part of a duo with John Abercrombie. They all showed up at our new home, Jan with bass player Palle Danielsson and pianist Bobo Stenson, and Ralph with John. It was an enjoyable evening, and everyone spent the night in our tiny house, sleeping on sofas and mattresses strewn all over the place – even in our cellar. One friend slept in my studio, behind the piano. A hippie-like idyll.

While free jazz was a movement, ECM became a kind of family. As a general rule, whoever joins ECM stays with ECM. In spite of its global success, the label has remained a small business. Everyone who works there can be classified as "slightly mad." Everyone is involved in Manfred Eicher's selection of musicians and productions. Everyone feels like they are part of the whole, thinking with it, working with it, contributing to it. When ECM musicians are in Germany, everyone gets together in the small office. I, too, still enjoy dropping by every now and then.

ECM cover art has been stylistically influential, receiving prizes on multiple occasions. The recording quality leaves nothing to be desired either. Eicher has created something truly special with ECM.

In the studio itself, there is no doubt that it is the big boss who calls the tune. Manfred Eicher embodies the ideal producer. He has an excellent ear, hearing even "fleas cough," and also knows the technical details required to reach perfection. He is a wonderful co-worker in the studio. But if he doesn't like the music being presented, you have a problem. He will only be fully invested in a production if it corresponds exactly to his standards. If there is a lack of synchronicity between the artist and the producer, you will need a lot of fortitude. You have to be absolutely sure of yourself, so it's advisable to appear in the studio fully prepared. Which is always a good idea anyway.

Figure 23: Keith Jarrett with Maja Weber; to the right, Thomas Stöwsand. ECM office, Munich, around 1974

10 Philharmonic Full Circle

I played at the Berlin Philharmonic Hall under my own name for the first time in the autumn of 1974, the same year my record with ECM was released – I had been invited to perform *The Colours of Chloë* at the jazz festival.

For this I put together a quartet with the two pianists Rainer Brüninghaus and Brian Miller, a Brit who had been recommended to me by a friend, the guitarist Gary Boyle. Ralf Hübner helped out on the drums. Then there was me, of course – and twelve cellists from the Berlin Opera. My one-hour production was to be played live for the first time.

Premiere at the Berlin Philharmonic Hall. Caution! Nightmare in sight! Back then, everything in Berlin had to align with the "spirit of freedom." Anything that wasn't labelled "free," was mercilessly booed. One basically couldn't show up with anything traditional – and here I was now, with twelve cellists, a conductor, a jazz quartet and two pianists! I knew the conductor, Mladen Gutesha, from SDR Stuttgart. When the institution of the "entertainment orchestra" was still in existence, he was a regular guest there. Early on, it was through him that I also met Chick Corea. He'd been recording a production with Gutesha and the entertainment orchestra in Stuttgart, when, once again, I was brought in as the telephone bassist.

Back to the Berlin premiere: things were going well for us. During the performance, the audience in the Berlin Philharmonic Hall was surprisingly quiet and attentive. I, however, was dreading the reaction of the "merciless." Then, something strange happened. The last note faded quietly – that alone was a provocation! Nothing. Silence. After what seemed like interminable moments of terror, I realized: the barrage of catcalls was about to be unleashed. Indeed, somewhere in the circle, I heard a timid "Boo." At the same time, though, sincere applause broke out, growing stronger and stronger, seemingly lasting forever, thunderous, roaring: I was ecstatic. It was a huge success. I chalked it all up to the unusual music – including the performance. Hardcore guests hadn't expected such "insolence." One review later wrote that twelve cellists had vanquished twelve tonnes of luggage – the American pianist Herbie Hancock had played after us, surrounded by a band that had arrived with an inordinate amount of equipment.

The host of the evening, ZDF's[1] Reinhard Knieper, took me to Hancock's dressing room before his performance. What ensued was a typically American use of compliments still unfamiliar to me back then. The question "Were you able to listen to Eberhard?" was answered by Herbie as follows: "No, sorry. I wasn't. I was preparing and had an interview myself."

Then he suddenly added: "But as a matter of fact, I could hear it through the wall. It was great!"

I thus became acquainted with American "friendliness" quite early on. As a rule, the dressing rooms in posh concert halls are expertly soundproofed. At best, you can only hear what is happening onstage via the miserable dressing-room speakers used by the stage manager to communicate with the performers.

To German ears, American friendliness often sounds insincere: "You're the best audience I've ever had!" How often have American singers and entertainers greeted their audience this way?

Americans don't seem to mind that the guy onstage starts his show with a big lie.

My initially rather poor knowledge of English caused great amusement on one occasion in New York when I took the greeting of the American ECM distributor quite literally. Feeling flattered by his "Nice to meet you!" I simply answered, "Thank you very much."

As is presumably the case for many other musicians, the Philharmonic Hall is a special place to me and a very special building even though it was designed by an anthroposophical architect who didn't focus on practical issues or ease of access. Whether a grand piano has to be lifted a flight of stairs every time it is needed is the kind of uninteresting fact that was sacrificed to ideology. It's no different at the Liederhalle in Stuttgart or the Philharmonic Hall in Munich. I find the Berlin Philharmonic Hall tedious when it comes to playing jazz. This is the case with many major concert halls. Famed for their outstanding acoustics, they were only conceived for classical music concerts. As soon as amplifiers come into play, natural mayhem follows. Nowadays good technical equipment and sound engineers are worth a great deal. But when it comes down to it, I never really felt comfortable at the Philharmonic Hall, not even as an audience member. It's odd – the concert hall in which my career as a band leader and composer began is the very last hall in which I stood onstage as a musician, even if it was just for a sound check.

---

1. *Zweites Deutsches Fernsehen* (Second German Television), a German public-service television broadcaster.

11 Well Received

America is the cradle of jazz, and American jazz musicians are the benchmark for the rest of the world. This held true for decades. And to some extent, it is still true today. We Europeans have to deem ourselves lucky if a little praise comes our way.

After the success of my first ECM recording, *The Colours of Chloë*, a number of American colleagues started to take notice of me: "Something new out of Europe? What's his name? Eberhard Faber?"

For my birthday, Paul McCandless even sent me a pencil with "Eberhard Faber" printed on it. Evidently, these Faber-Castell pencils were popular in the US back then – I didn't immediately get the joke that in American English my name is pronounced almost like the pencil brand.

"It could be worth a try!" This is what Ralph Towner and Gary Burton may have thought when they invited me to recording sessions – Ralph to *Solstice* and later to *Sound and Shadows*, Gary to *Ring* and then to *Passengers*. You can imagine what it meant to me to be invited by Gary Burton to join a tour with his quintet in the USA. While my chest swelled with pride, I thought: "Will I manage to meet expectations?" But this question should have been: "Will I manage to reach perfection?"

There is no doubt that the USA regularly produces a wealth of talent. The numbers Gary Burton once shared with me at his Berklee College of Music are staggering. Apparently, in his day, there were 5000 guitar and bass students a year – even the number of vibraphone students reached 1200. Incredible! All of the other instruments boasted equally spectacular statistics.

With such a glut of music students, one can't help but wonder: where are they all going to play? Even if a large percentage of beginners never complete their studies and end up with more ordinary jobs, in the US, the competition among jazz musicians is significantly stiffer than in comparatively cosy Europe. After all, even in the US, it can't be expected that more than one or two Berklee graduates a year shoot to fame and manage to make ends meet with a more or less decent salary.

Figure 24: Eberhard Weber with Paul McCandless around 1980

As a musician, you face far more pressure in the States than in the Old World because you can't ignore how many talented people there are to begin with. Probationary periods in orchestras or bands exist solely to check if you are a good fit. Perfect technique is a given. Errors can be made once. The second time, a raised eyebrow indicates: "There won't be a third." Still, knowing that everyone is playing to the best of their ability is refreshing. After all, the next candidate is already waiting at the door, optimally prepared.

This is how Pat Metheny's career started. An ardent admirer of Gary Burton, he had studied all the pieces in Gary's current programmes – just in case Gary might suddenly need a guitarist. Pat would have been ready at any given moment. And indeed, the moment came when the band was due for a shake-up. Pat was able to step in with ease. And he was successful. I witnessed it myself when Gary invited me to join the tour. This very young guitarist with long hair and hardly any experience got onstage, beaming. Then he started to play the whole programme, effortlessly, with an astounding degree of precision: this is what Pat is like. The way he played was refreshingly easy-going. He blended in without needing any time to warm up, without missing any entries – very American.

I also witnessed the level of professionalism that existed in the studio. During a recording session, Gary once said to Steve Swallow: "In this piece you're playing a solo – just one chorus. Better be good! We're not repeating it!"

This sort of announcement would have made us Europeans shrink in horror. How is this supposed to work? You can't produce anything decent under this much pressure. But Steve played impeccably, flawlessly. Perfect, as always. It was a wrap!

I had the advantage of being a guest soloist. No one wants to throw out their guests. The worst that can happen to a guest is that they won't be invited again. In the 1950s, just as I was beginning to dream of a career as a professional musician, I had no inkling of anything resembling competition. You could find it in business – but in culture? Today I know that you're even more likely to encounter it there.

Why did Gary Burton have an Eberhard Weber flown in from Europe? I found out that back then a lawyer had to be engaged so that I would be granted the authorization to play. Cost: around 1000 US dollars. I had to pick up my visa in person at an American consulate in Germany. The only way European musicians could perform in the States back then was with hard-to-obtain work permits. At the American consulate in Frankfurt, I was once given an unusual introduction. As always, I had been waiting in the waiting room with many other visitors. An elderly consular official appeared in the room from time to time, calling out a name. After handing out some paperwork, he would disappear again. Eventually, he returned: "Eberhard Weber?"

I got up.

Pointing at me, he cried out excitedly: "Ladies and Gentlemen, one of the greatest bass players in the world!"

In Munich, I had a very different experience. A young staff member without any knowledge of the jazz scene was responsible for my visa application. She was an expert in the field of opera singing – and simply denied my application: "I know all of the singers. I'm not familiar with a bass player by the name of Eberhard Weber."

Jan Garbarek, on the other hand, was granted the authorization to play in the US on the sole grounds that he had been declared a gift of the Norwegian king to the American people on the occasion of bicentennial celebrations.

When I was invited by Gary Burton, Steve Swallow was the bassist in his quintet. Two bass players in one band? What was that about? That couldn't go well. Gary Burton's idea to have me join his quintet couldn't have had anything to do with him being a proven bass fan who insisted on having two bass players in one band. Low frequencies are much too tricky for this; rather than illuminate, they are more likely to obfuscate things.

No one – except perhaps a couple of "*free*booters" – would ever think of using two basses on an equal footing. Surely, my being booked was due to the fact that there was a bass player in Europe, at Gary's label ECM at that, who made solo parts on his instrument possible while avoiding the confusing low frequencies. It was clear from the get-go: I had been booked on account of my improvisations on this new, rather unusual construct.

All the same, from an acoustic point of view, two basses represented more than a gamble. When low-pitched sounds come together, they have the tendency to "crumble" or fragment, to sound indistinct and blurry. Steve and I analysed and solved the problem of potentially diffuse sound by agreeing ahead of time who would go up high and who would stay low at any given moment. Neither of us would have ever thought: "I'll do the dirty on my colleague, I'll play to win."

After years of experience, we both knew that war onstage is sheer nonsense. Cooperation alone leads to the end goal – or to anything viable, at least. Anyone who is experienced feels at once that power struggles are based on foolishness.

I always enjoyed playing, but not rehearsing. Perhaps this was an early indication of my penchant for improvisation. Improvisation allows for self-representation without demanding too much in terms of technique. I never prepared spontaneous solos. In all my years onstage, there were very few occasions on which I decided it would be better to know in advance what I wanted people to hear. You have to know yourself well enough to decide whether it is worth the risk or better to "play it safe." I always preferred the risk. I didn't like the motto: "Yesterday, this solo brought the house down, so why not simply repeat it today?" Apparently, there really are fans who follow a band around to hear exactly the same thing played again. Listening intently isn't everyone's thing. So why torture oneself onstage when one could have it easy? I still preferred the risk. I didn't feel like churning out the same thing every night. In the long run, relying on my ingenuity night after night served me quite well.

I loved the moment it was my turn. Go for it! Pick up from where? From my predecessor's key? Leave it to chance? Which note or chord would be worthwhile? Play it snappy or smooth? Throw in a surprise? Or something to be expected? Naturally, these deliberations take some time for the brain to process. But it's my turn. I can't pause for effect. Any considerations taken into account while playing effectively take place after one has started playing. Is it better to "let it rip" or to tug at the heartstrings? I have already asked the question in a previous chapter: why play five choruses instead of just two or three? Regarding unaccompanied solos, there are no rules anyway. The solo is a process of auto-inspiration, of seeking and finding, a mix of reflection and intuition. An independent, spontaneous composition is to be created.

The more I think about it and try to put the genesis of a solo into words, the more I realize that no two nights are ever the same.

For the listener, it is incredibly difficult to follow a series of dull sounds, especially if they aren't supported by harmonically accompanied chords. If one has missed the start of a bass solo, who can immediately say which point in the composition the bass player has reached? Complicating things further is the fact that there aren't too many bass players who can convey acoustic clarity in especially low or fast sequences of notes. It could also be due to the fact that in the lower registers on the contrabass no vibrations can physically emerge in a way that would make it possible for the human ear to detect the intention of the player.

But you learn very quickly how to impress your public – even how to render it speechless. Naturally, this holds true for all instruments. Any experienced performer is intimately familiar with the limitations of their own instrument. Certain types of success are dependent on the instrument. With the trumpet, it's how high you can go; with many other instruments, it's the number of notes you can play; with the drums, it's how loud you can get. Every thunderous outburst is met with rapturous applause. Inevitable and intentional. And then there's speed: speed always seems to guarantee exhilaration.

Bass players have an invaluable advantage: they never get the root note wrong. If the chord is "through" after the first chorus, you can think about what else works with it from the second. You just have to make sure the nature of the chord isn't ruined by abandoning the root note. Under these circumstances, it may happen that the same boring root note has to be used over and over again with each repetition, unless a fellow player takes mercy and temporarily takes over this task. Still, abandoning the root note once can definitely be seen as a diversion, as creativity.

I had a different kind of experience during a performance in Hamburg's Fabrik. It was an NDR concert. Michael Naura, who was head of the jazz department back then, had put together a duo: Ack van Rooyen on trumpet and flugelhorn, and Wolfgang Dauner on piano. Contrary to the original intention, Naura decided to add a bass to the duo after all. I must have been in the area at the time, so I was "added on." I was used to Wolfgang giving me, the bass, space. That's how it had been for years. However, we hadn't played together for several years at this point, ever since I'd moved on to the Dave Pike Set and Kriegel's Spectrum. Now, in Hamburg, I was soon at a loss because Wolfgang took away my function as a bass by occupying all the low notes with his left hand. As described earlier, low-pitched sounds are virtually impossible to combine without having them merge in a blur. On top of that, the low notes sound much clearer on the piano than on the double bass. Dauner's hand was rigorously occupying my region. Had we rehearsed ahead of time, we would have noticed. But since we got onstage spontaneously, there was nothing I could do. Wolfgang pulled through his powerful accompaniment, failing to acknowledge how helpless, how superfluous I felt. I have no idea if by bringing me onboard Naura had acted on his own authority, thereby provoking my colleagues. Did they want to bring this to my attention? In the end, this night, too, passed without leaving any scars.

Figure 25: Michael DiPasqua, Paul McCandless, Eberhard Weber, Bill Frisell, Lyle Mays; NDR Studio, Hamburg, 1982

What is certain as far as I am concerned is that root notes are important – everything else is based on them. That's why I am a staunch supporter of a clearly audible bass: a chord or a key's character is critical when it comes to determining the nature of the sound. With slower compositions, any bass that can be played decently allows the harmony to be perceived. If things speed up, however, it becomes increasingly difficult to sustain the root note system. It's at this point, at the latest, that experience and routine are required, and, in many cases, an instrument that doesn't tolerate any dull vagueness. Electronic instruments – synthesizers, electric pianos or any other sustained sound options – can provide bassists with freedom, and support their creative urges, their urge to shine. At this point, other notes on the harmonic scale can be introduced without worry. This was the great advantage of playing in the Gary Burton Quintet with Steve Swallow: when I took off, he kept the harmonic structure together.

The tour kicked off in Philadelphia. This was the first time I had set foot on American soil, and I was completely unsure of what to expect. Back then, German television was still full of horror stories, and a journey to the new world was a journey into the unknown. Attacks, murders, shootings. Six people killed every day in New York alone; in Chicago, it was eight on average. And in Philadelphia? Was it safe? Could you walk down the street without being harmed? How did you survive in the US as a jazz musician? There was much to take into account in the new world. I'd heard of the bass player David Izenzon's tragic fate. He'd left a jazz club with his bass early in the morning, then put it down briefly to unlock his car. When he turned around, he saw a guy running away with his instrument. David frantically chased after him – and suffered a fatal heart attack.

Here is another story, less tragic: various ECM bands met up one afternoon in Boston to set up for a rehearsal in a hall. I was already on location and had unpacked my gear when Jack DeJohnette appeared in the hall, greeting us with a big hello – we hadn't seen each other in a long time. When he went back outside to unload, his car was empty: everything had been stolen. I became acquainted with American reality fast – Gary Burton, who had also just arrived, immediately remarked: "How can you leave your instruments out of sight in a big city, even if it's just for a few moments?" That is to say, from an American point of view, he made Jack alone responsible for the disaster – a bit confusing for me, as a European. But there was scepticism on both sides. A dear colleague of Jewish descent, Danny Gottlieb, full of concern before a trip to Germany, once asked me: "Is it still dangerous in Germany for a Jew?" To this day we have both survived various trips across the continents unscathed.

My first US tour involved a fair amount of anguish. Not only was I going to be performing in the USA for the first time, I also had to live up to a lot of propagandistic groundwork. ECM had hyped me up in the media. Somehow, it seemed to have worked – interviews were being requested en masse. In the beginning, I was still excited about every radio station's offer of a live interview. In Germany, there were only about ten stations in the whole country back then. I never would have expected there to be hundreds in the US, pressing me to give interviews as soon as I performed in their respective broadcasting area. To protect myself, I eventually had no choice but to tell the American ECM representative to only accept interviews with a small selection of major broadcasters. What struck me as odd back then was that towards the end of each interview I was asked to make an announcement along the lines of: "Hi, I'm Eberhard Weber, and I listen to WKFX, my favourite radio station."

Nobody seemed interested in the fact that I was in the States for the first time. I imagine that even to the listeners it must have seemed highly unlikely that of all stations I would listen to WKFX.

Just being good wasn't enough now. I had to be convincing, I had to prove that I'd been invited with good reason, that there was something special in my instrument case. To be one of many, and potentially interchangeable – that was insufficient. It would have been good if I'd grown up the American way, up against stiff competition, and not so nonchalantly European. But it was too late now – I was thrown into the American jazz business, and more than survival, I wanted victory. I wanted to astonish.

So there I was in "Phili," having to set up onstage as soon as I arrived. I had recorded two LPs with Gary for ECM, so there were already about ten tracks I had down pat. The hitch was that I should have been able to play and perform twice as many. I placed the notes in front of me, the Real Book always at hand. Two of my compositions had made their way into volumes one and two of the then legendary Real Book: *The Colours of Chloë* and *Yellow Fields.* At the time, I was the only German to have managed this. These Real Books were popular with musicians because in their pages, jazz standards, as well as better-known new compositions, could be found in the form of lead sheets, which made it possible to play them. Interestingly enough, these publications, often handwritten, were illegal. Naturally, the holders of the rights weren't happy about them. Nowadays, newer – legalized – versions are available with significantly better transcriptions and less handwriting.

Gary specified which composition in the Real Book would be played. But there was no time to rehearse. In spite of this, it would have to be presented as perfectly as if it had been part of our repertoire for ages – not as if I had just flipped open the book. It's fun to interpret something this way, without anyone in the audience noticing.

This being my first visit to the USA, I was so impressed, that I kept a kind of diary, recording where and when I played, in which hall, what the hall or club looked like, and how big the audience was. I wrote everything down – for whom? Who would ever benefit from the knowledge that I once performed my composition 'The Colours of Chloë' with Gary Burton's band in a hall with golden candelabra in front of around 400 spectators? Back then I was filled with pride. Hold on to everything! Don't forget a thing! Now that I could actually use these notes – which no one's ever read – they have disappeared. Most likely, I threw them away myself on one of the many occasions I moved house. By the second time Gary Burton invited me, a sense of routine started to seep in, the initial euphoria evaporated, and nothing was documented anymore. I was wholly occupied with the humdrum of touring.

Gary led his formation perfectly, thinking of every eventuality ahead of time. A rented trailer for our instruments and luggage was attached to his personal van. We drove from state to state, for hundreds of miles, criss-crossing North America from the East Coast to the West Coast, through the Midwest, to the north of Canada, and the south of Texas. I think Alaska is the only state I never visited. What was interesting for me, being European, is that our hotels were always on the city limits, and never at the centre. The reason for this is obvious: in the centre, there was hardly ever any space to park, let alone for a cumbersome trailer. As a result, we'd often spend the night near a shopping centre with a giant carpark. Safety first, though: Gary always got a room with a view of the parking lot and our vehicle, so he could intervene just in case any thieves tried their luck.

Aside from that, I noticed that many American drivers had trouble driving in reverse. This must have something to do with the size of the country and its parking lots. There was an abundance of space, with easy vehicle access. During one of the later US tours with my band Colours, our professional roadie proved incapable of manoeuvring his own bus into a narrow alley in Washington, D.C. Unfortunately, this happened to be the only way of reaching our club, the Blues Alley, to load and unload our equipment.

During my first US tour with Gary, I also met Eddie Gomez, another fantastic colleague on the bass. One of my compositions, 'The Colours of Chloë', featured in the programme. We had got set up, I was sitting onstage in front of the band, directly facing the audience, no more than two metres away from the front row. Before the concert, Eddie Gomez had visited us in our dressing room, and Gary had introduced me. To my great – but regrettably, also temporary – joy, I noticed Eddie sitting diagonally across from me in the first row. I felt no fear performing in front of my famous American colleague – slight tension, at most.

We played 'The Colours of Chloë'. After Gary's introductory bars, it was my turn. I had to play the first melody with the bow. I reached for it, placed it on the strings – and it slipped out of my hand, rolling forward until it landed in front of someone sitting in the first row. The helpful audience-member picked it up and handed it to me onstage. There is nothing else to say about the incident. Except that I would have liked to have had access to a trapdoor.

Apart from this, I rarely had the chance to meet renowned colleagues, bass players in my case. It's not for nothing that the doubling of instruments is called a "battle" in the jargon of hosts and presenters. Bass battles are particularly bad because, as already mentioned, low frequencies are the least suited to pairing. Who did I get to know? Who not? What does it even mean "to know"? Among bass players you hardly ever get to know your colleagues because you're hardly ever on the road together – blinkered specialists prevail.

In person I have met Stanley Clarke, Niels-Henning Ørsted Pedersen, Charlie Haden, Gary Peacock, Dave Holland, John Patitucci, Glen Moore, David Friesen, Mark Egan, Marc Johnson, Miroslav Vitous, Palle Danielsson and Arild Andersen – all listed here for "the encyclopaedia."

I also came to know, and appreciate, Steve Swallow – we were on the road together with Gary Burton for weeks.

Jaco Pastorius, on the other hand, I never got to meet. Though we both tried. This is how: during a US tour I was told that Jaco had called. I called back. No answer. Much later, back in Germany, I heard from a promoter that Weather Report were going to guest at Circus Krone in Munich. At the time, Jaco was Zawinul and Shorter's bassist. This was my chance: in addition to my two tickets, I got a backstage pass so that I would finally be able to meet Jaco in person after the show. Maja and I had the worst seats in the whole rotunda – by far. We could hardly see the stage and the sound was awful. The band played a new set that I, as a Weather Report fan, wasn't familiar with yet. Although I have a decent pair of ears, I simply couldn't make out what was being blasted from the stage.

After a brief discussion with my equally frustrated wife, we decided to put an end to our misery. As cautiously as we could, we got up and moved through the narrow rows of seats towards the exit. It was as cramped and unpleasant for us as for the other audience members. More uncomfortable yet was the fact that I was well known in Munich at the time. Not only did people know who Eberhard Weber was, they also knew what he looked like. As we fought our way through the rows, the music suddenly died down – Jaco Pastorius was about to start his big solo. What were we to do now? Stay put? Fight our way back? Sit on someone's lap? We opted to keep pushing forward so as to end the ordeal as soon as possible.

That was my "encounter" with Jaco Pastorius. Shortly thereafter he was beaten up by a bouncer outside a jazz club in New York and died of his injuries.

12 "Now you've made it!"

Unquestionably, *The Colours of Chloë* was my springboard. The prize was awarded, the debut at the Berlin Jazz Festival a success, the LP on the market – more records had to be pressed fast. The first 3000 had been sold in no time. Who'd have thought? Certainly not I, and most likely ECM hadn't expected such a great success, either. Naturally, we wanted to keep it up, and tried to put together a live band we could tour with. Back then I still wanted to see the world, discover new things, become famous. I wanted to show what great music was waiting to be disseminated. As far as I can recall, money was not a driving factor. I needed a band that could travel. It had to include a piano, a keyboard and a drummer, and myself as the bass player. A second pianist, like at the Berlin Philharmonic Hall? Undoable! Two pianos were too complicated for the scene we expected. It was clear to me that we would have to start small – in clubs which, as a rule, didn't have two pianos. Two Fender Rhodes? One would be enough to break our backs while transporting it! Roadies were as unthinkable at that point as great concert halls with two pianos. What was the solution?

It began with the answer to the easiest question: who would the pianist be? Rainer Brüninghaus and I had decided long ago that we would stay together after leaving Spectrum. So, Rainer was in. We got along both personally and musically.

The drummer – who could it be? Through ECM I met their preferred drummer Jon Christensen. The way he played was very modern. Quick and mellow, Jon played the cymbals as only Jack DeJohnette could. And Jon was game.

Now for the wind player. Who was a good match for a quartet? All considerations ended with the realization that all of the top picks were unavailable. Initially I thought of a Scandinavian saxophone player – after all, we already had a Norwegian, Jon, on the drums. Names were mentioned, recommendations made. One was Charlie Mariano – he'd just arrived from the States at the time and intended to stay in Germany. I was unsure at first because I didn't want any big names. I wanted a band of equals among equals. After many discussions, which, by the way, included Volker Kriegel – hereby countering the rumour that we had fallen out – I conceded that an older, more experienced American carthorse might be quite useful in helping us pull together. Too bad that I didn't particularly like Charlie's favourite instrument, the alto sax. I'll never find out why Charlie gave in, playing only the soprano with Colours – and now and then even the exotic Indian nagaswaram. At any rate, Charlie loved our band – and as an old hand, he probably realized that the soprano saxophone worked better here than the alto, which is more commonly associated with the blues.

Figure 26: Eberhard Weber and Charlie Mariano in the late 1970s

We were all set. It was 1976 and all I needed now was a repertoire, which meant I had to compose. At least I was spared the tedious E flat transposition of the alto sax. Like the tenor sax, the soprano only requires the simpler B flat transposition, which is tedious enough as it is… Those who know me, know that I deliver only the bare necessities and refuse to waste resources on preparations "for every eventuality." This meant that I only wrote enough compositions to fill one hour twice. Alright – I concede that I wrote two more for encores. But that was it.

Since he'd arrived in Germany, Charlie had been represented by Vera Brandes, the music manager from Cologne, so it was quite natural for her to become our first agent, too. She did a good job. It wasn't long before we went on our first German tours. Under the name Colours, the band released its first record with ECM, *Yellow Fields*. It had just hit the market when Jon unexpectedly left the band. I never found out why. To replace him, I asked John Marshall if he would join us – I knew the Briton from the Kriegel LP *Missing Link*. He agreed at once and stayed with us until the band split up in the winter of 1981. But back then the end wasn't yet in sight.

I can't put it any other way: things kept getting better. Our growing success was echoed by the size of the halls we performed in. Soon enough, we were playing in Switzerland and Austria. We also went on a short tour of the GDR. We were exotic there with our button-down shirts and jeans and the posh red Mercedes bus we'd rented to transport our equipment. Although we were paid in East German marks, back in the West, we received a subsidy in western Deutschmarks: the eastern currency couldn't be exported. It had to be spent, which wouldn't have been a problem – had there been anything to buy.

On Charlie's birthday, I tried to get him some flowers – his German girl-friend had asked me to, and I was happy to oblige. As it happened, there was a florist across from our hotel. But when I crossed the street, I was faced with an endless queue. There was nothing to do but join it. Surprisingly, it didn't take very long until it was my turn. The reason soon became clear: there was only one kind of flower for sale. I'd never seen a florist so empty! Through some sort of miracle, I was able to buy the last bouquet. The people in line behind me didn't moan, though – they had to be used to it.

What could we do with our East German money if we couldn't blow it? When a lack of single rooms was discreetly alluded to by our hotel's management, it sounded like this: "Gentlemen, don't you know each other well? Surely, you wouldn't mind sharing a twin room?"

With lightning speed, we mutated into capitalists: "Are your suites still available? The honeymoon suite? The presidential suite?"

Checking.

"Yes."

"We'll take them."

"But they're considerably more... erm..."

"No problem!"

Gradually, we managed to rid ourselves of our GDR riches. We repeated this embarrassing performance when we discovered one of the few interesting goods for sale – records. We had various assortments presented to us: Russian classical music, local folk, eastern jazz. We bought it all.

"Don't you have anything else?"

"You've just bought goods worth more than a monthly wage!"

As Colours grew in popularity, our wages, too, grew more handsome. According to the press, we were now the most famous band in Europe, an accolade previously bestowed on Ian Carrs' Nucleus, a band in which John

Marshall played the drums. Before that, he had been part of Soft Machine, "the most famous band that never played," as he used to complain.

With Colours, we really did start to travel the world. Not that Europe was covered – we just happened to get offers from elsewhere, first from the USA. By then, I was well known there, mainly due to ECM's good marketing and the presence of my LPs on the American market. Back then, there were record stores à gogo – and I could be found in their jazz sections, in a category of my own.

We played in the US several times with Colours, once as the opening act for Oregon, Ralph Towner and Paul McCandless's band. It is customary that the first band to play carries out its sound check last in order to avoid unnecessary reconversions. Consequently, Oregon did their sound check first. They were painstakingly precise: not once during the two-week tour did we find the time to fine-tune our sound to a similar degree. The Oregonians checked every single instrument – four times over. Each member of the quartet assessed the sound both onstage and from the audience. This took so long that we, as the opening act, had no more than ten minutes left to carry out our own sound check because eventually the audience would request admission. We had no choice but to adjust our sound within earshot of the entering audience members. Such is the lot of the opening act. As band leader I didn't want to intervene. We were all friends and I didn't want to ruffle any feathers. I just kept hoping that Oregon would notice that we didn't have enough time.

Oh well. It didn't stop us from being successful and coming off well. And we are still friends today. And I won't hide that it felt incredibly good to be one of the few German musicians to have "made it" in the US, too. Back then, at the end of the twentieth century.

As I write these words, I am reminded of the first time I received this compliment. Actually, I can't relate the occasion because, once again, I am not in the position to trace back its time or exact circumstances. Let me try anyway: Volker Kriegel must have just founded Spectrum when, for reasons unknown, I received the offer to arrange a few of my compositions for a string orchestra from Lake Constance and perform them there. I was accompanied by the roadie Walter Pauly, who helped me with the setup. Over deafening applause at the end of the concert, he turned to me, saying: "Now you've made it!"

In 1976 there was also something like an ECM tour through the US, consisting exclusively of musicians and bands that belonged to the "stable." Hailing from Europe, there was Terje Rypdal with Palle Danielsson, and then me, with Colours. Our "local" stablemates were Gary Burton and his quintet – with me as their guest soloist. Additionally, there was the guitar duo comprising John Abercrombie and Ralph Towner – and, as the grand finale, Keith Jarrett's American Quartet with, if I remember correctly, Charlie Haden on bass, Paul Motian on drums and Dewey Redman on tenor saxophone.

One concert stands out vividly in my recollection because right from the start the musicians and event organizers were in a state of turmoil. It took place in New York's Avery Fisher Hall, a venue better suited for classical music. We were all informed that, come what may, we would have to respect the allotted play time by the minute. Should the concert fail to end by exactly eleven o'clock, all incurring fees would be charged a second time: room rental, stage personnel, dressers – everything. And as we were told, the Avery Fisher Hall is far from cheap. One thing was clear to us all: we would have to prevent acts from overrunning and watch out for encores, always a potential source of problems. Things kicked off on time with the Abercrombie / Towner Duo. We were all gathered behind the stage, listening closely. They played. And played. And played. They announced another piece, and played some more. Careful! The agreed-on thirty minutes were over now. This wasn't exactly unusual. You can't make the audience responsible for organizational issues – an encore had to be performed. At this point, however, something totally unexpected happened. The two musicians had a surprise guest, the percussionist Collin Walcott, join them onstage for the encore. Wild enthusiasm! The crowd demanded more encores.

Figure 27: Outdoor advertising for Eberhard Weber and his band Colours in Eau Claire, Wisconsin, in the late 1970s

Gradually, an entirely justified sense of unease started developing backstage. The thirty minutes had ended ages ago! What the heck? We started sending signs through the side curtains reading "STOP!" We never found out what moved the three musicians to play for well over an hour. All the other bands had to cut their time short so as to respect the curfew. Colours played for half of the originally agreed-on time, as did Burton. In spite of this, no more than eight minutes were left for the last act – the Keith Jarrett Quartet! To say we were all "absolutely livid" would be a gross understatement: no one wanted to talk to the Abercrombie / Towner Duo and their surprise guest for the rest of the tour!

Still, at least Colours got to play at the Avery Fisher Hall – in New York – even if it was just for twenty minutes. Things were more civilized in the other cities we travelled to, like Boston, St. Louis, Detroit, San Francisco and Los Angeles. There even came a time when we all talked to each other again.

13 Down Under

After my first tour with Gary Burton, I was proud of the fact that I was accepted not only by the American public, but also by my new colleagues. In the following years, I regularly travelled to the States, often twice a year. Soon my presence in the land of boundless opportunity also became evident in the charts. In polls conducted by jazz magazines, I regularly topped the category "Talent Deserving Wider Recognition" (TDWR). Later I even made it into the category of established musicians: 1. Jaco Pastorius, 2. Stanley Clarke, 3. Eberhard Weber, 4. Steve Swallow. It still feels good to have been a part of this circle of select bass players, even if today there are no material benefits involved. It also feels good because it confirms a theory of mine: individuality matters more than technical perfection. Years ago, it was normal to engage studio musicians for comping purposes. Not just string and wind ensembles, but also drummers and bass players. Nowadays, almost everything can be obtained at the touch of a button, programmed by Sony, Yamaha or Logic. It's amazing what sounds can be produced industrially these days, almost indistinguishable from the real thing. The so-called samplers are based on genuine, real instruments, which, once they have been neatly recorded, can be retrieved at the touch of a key.

Only the soloistic remains the prerogative of the individual, although the soloistic must be distinguished from the solo here. A melody on the trumpet certainly can be "programmed." But the improvised, manipulated, dynamic and personal is not programmable. A true soloist will always be idiosyncratic, peculiar – and hopefully always inimitable. Many a reader may remember that I was once viciously attacked for having advocated in a printed interview that "Jazz is dead." This prompted an industry-wide outcry, I was reviled, accused of senility. What I said next, however, was overlooked: "Long live improvisation!" What really matters is that creativity and spontaneity survive – during *live* performances.

Compared to rock and pop music, jazz remained free from glamour back then. Nothing against that. Still, a certain degree of name recognition did bring about some rather odd situations. Once, as I was waiting at the airport for my flight out of Madrid to depart, a man approached me, addressing me in German: "Are you Eberhard Weber?"

"Yes," I replied. On that, the gentleman abruptly turned away and disappeared without saying a word.

Another time, on a domestic flight, a stewardess approached me with a piece of paper, handing it to me almost shyly: "Could I ask you for an autograph, Herr Dauner?"

On yet another occasion, Ev Kriegel, my guitarist friend Volker's widow, told me that while she had been sunbathing on a beach somewhere in California, a young man started a conversation with her. "Where are you from?" he asked.

When Ev replied, "I'm German," he said, "Oh, Germany – Eberhard Weber!" not knowing that Ev and I knew each other.

Would I be writing down these anecdotes if I didn't enjoy remembering them to a certain extent? Over the course of forty years, I also received quite a bit of fan mail. Among it were two very moving letters – one from the US, another from Sweden. Both senders wrote that they had been severely depressed – just about to commit suicide. Then they heard my music, which they said gave them so much, that they distanced themselves from their plan. This is what they wanted to thank me for.

These letters made me very happy back then, and I immediately wrote back to the formerly suicidal writers. I can only hope that the effect my music had on them was sustained. Naturally, no one ever wrote to let me know if my music had the opposite effect.

In the US I really couldn't complain about a lack of recognition. Although I rarely went back in later years, I was able to sustain a high profile there thanks to the unexpected status provided by ECM's global sales.

On returning to Germany, these tours always elicited questions. What was different in the US? What differences were there between German and American musicians? Many things are the same. But although there is massive competition there, crippling competition, there is no envy or jealousy – unlike on our side of the planet. Whoever works hard in the States is entitled to creaming off, to earning more. It's part of the system. Business comes first – the Salvation Army has other duties. You just know it's better to be a part of things and not to get pushed aside. That's why you fight, constantly, always giving your best, fully concentrated every second. "I have a headache, a fever, blisters on my fingers, I'm under the weather!" Not once did I hear any of these excuses or explanations in the US.

Figure 28: Eberhard Weber with Charlie Mariano, John Marshall and Rainer Brüninghaus on a concert poster in Australia, 1981

In the music industry, too, business as usual is the norm: if you can't keep up, you're dropped. It's that simple. The show must go on – without "feeble" excuses. "Outside," the healthy await their turn without complaints or limitations, fully prepared. Your shortcomings are their delight. I remember a practice session with the United Jazz + Rock Ensemble when Charlie Mariano was rehearsing his new composition with us. I have rarely seen anyone as impatient as Charlie when things aren't played flawlessly right from the start. His fast-paced piece was fairly complicated and certainly could have been played more slowly the first time around. But Charlie immediately set a very brisk pace. When chaos ensued, he stopped the ensemble right away and repeated the piece at the same breakneck tempo. We were all pros. But Charlie, being American, was a bit more of a pro, a fact he conveyed clearly with his constant rehearsals, perhaps quite deliberately. European leisureliness wasn't his thing.

What remains to be seen is which is better. Which is more effective? The tough American way or our usual European measuredness? There is no doubt as to which is more comfortable. But there is a certain appeal to everything holding water from the get-go, and not requiring ten attempts. I admit it is a blessing when a fair number of musicians have a composition down pat the very first time. The most satisfying experience was to get in on the act from the start without having to ask for a repeat "from bar twenty-four, please," and again "from bar one hundred and eighteen." There is a real difference between repeating something to fine-tune it stylistically and doing so to correct simple errors.

The tours with Gary Burton and his crew became routine before long, no different from tours in Germany: you woke up at the hotel, drove to the gig, got set up, gave your concert, wrapped things up and drove back to the hotel. Another day, another destination. You did your job, listened to your colleagues, waited for agreed-on signs. After years in the business, only out-of-the-ordinary events still managed to irritate: a broken instrument or static coming from an amp. But your colleagues' performance was a given: everyone played terrifically, always. How could I still conjure up the enthusiasm and anticipation of the concertgoers? Gary Burton played masterfully, Steve Swallow was always accurate and reliable, and Pat Metheny was in the process of slowly developing a solo career in the hopes of leading a band of his own. The drummer couldn't stand hermetically sealed windows, so he often changed hotels. The workaday life of pros on tour. Except that in the US, it went on for weeks on end. On the rare occasion that we did have a day off and didn't need to play, we sat together, talked, asked each other questions, played games, and ate out – mostly fast food, consumed in a hurry.

Figure 29: As billed on a concert poster during the Australian tour: Eberhard Weber and Colours

A few years later, Colours was invited to Australia and New Zealand. The band had been around for six years by then, and I started to sense a certain fatigue, both as a band leader and a composer. I noticed issues in the band similar to the ones I'd been responsible for with Spectrum. Divisions became palpable, it felt like things were falling apart, and I wasn't in the mood to worry about it anymore. Rainer was "ripe," he wanted to do his own thing. Once in a while he'd play provocatively, which was basically OK. Things weren't set in stone: there was enough leeway. However, when Rainer played a unison melody on Charlie's saxophone one semitone higher, it may well have sounded interesting and daring, but it became more and more obvious that we were drifting apart. He wanted to do something that was his own instead of always playing for others. Added to that was the fact that three of our wives had accompanied us down under. To put it tactfully, there were little jealousies, arguments, spats. The feeling I had back then was that I'd had enough. But I was too cowardly to tell the band then and there that we would pack it in after the Australian tour. Instead, I said: "We're going to take a long break." And that's exactly what we did. In fact, we are still on our break today.

Still, Colours stands for a wonderful, successful time in my life. Years later, Charlie Mariano said to me: "Why did you stop that band? It was so great!" He'd never said that before, when we were still working together. To the contrary, he'd often seemed strangely detached. When decisions had to be made, his only comment used to be: "I don't care!"

Oddly enough, during the six years of the band's existence, he only ever played using sheet music, unlike the rest of us, who memorized everything. On one awkward occasion – I think it was in Belgium – I had to go backstage to get him the score during a live radio broadcast. The announcer had just introduced us when Charlie turned to me, saying: "Music?" What he really meant was: "The score!" The live broadcast started with a couple of minutes' silence.

14 Longer than Most Marriages

Jan Garbarek called me just a few days after we got back from Australia. Did I want to play in his new band? Yes! That was just the ticket: getting back onstage without too long of a break after Colours – and not having to be in charge anymore, getting a chance to recharge my batteries to boot. Evidently, I was more than ready to give up the role of band leader.

What wasn't clear yet was who would be a part of the new quartet. Along with Keith Jarrett, Jan had become a superstar of the jazz scene. Having just returned from several long tours with Jarrett, Jon Christensen and Palle Danielsson, Jan indicated that as a great Jarrett fan himself, he preferred not to have a pianist in his band at all: Jarrett was one-of-a-kind, inimitable.

I'd just met an American guitarist, called Bill Frisell. He'd come from Boston with Mike Gibbs, the composition teacher at Berklee College. I met Bill after Mike invited me to go on tour with an English big band in the UK. I'm certainly no discoverer, but it was immediately obvious to me that Bill was special. I subsequently booked him for a few duo concerts with me and he totally won me over. I therefore recommended him to Jan Garbarek, who was very keen. Add Jon Christensen on the drums, and we had a great quartet!

But we'd hardly finished recording the Jan Garbarek Group's first LP when Jon Christensen left the band. His motive remains unknown. I now called Michael DiPasqua into play. Jan agreed, and the band was whole again. Suddenly, however, Bill Frisell informed us that he would rather play with his mentor, the drummer Paul Motian. All of our efforts to change Bill's mind were in vain.

At this point one attempt followed the next, initially with two American guitarists. First Ross Trout, a studio guitarist from Chicago, then David Torn from the Everyman Band – each with a story of their own. Then it was our first pianist's turn, the Swede Lars Jansson. Like many pianists, he complained about having to play the keyboards rather than the queen of instruments, the grand piano. Yet this was Jan's express wish. Eventually I brought Rainer

Brüninghaus into the band. After roughly eleven different constellations, things finally fell into place – notwithstanding the occasional toing and froing on the drums and percussion.

By then I'd managed to bring so much onto the stage that I didn't need to worry about being relegated to the sidelines. I'd become much more assertive and knew how to defend myself. Colours had kept me completely satisfied for six years. I'd been able to compose and learn how to develop a band's sound. I'd also learned what it takes to knock the socks off the audience – without speedy, show-stopping phrases and arrangements designed to make the listeners jump up and down. I didn't want to settle for cheap sensationalism. I'd managed to make Weber distinctive, instantly recognizable as Weber.

In the beginning, almost anything was possible in the Jan Garbarek Group. The concept remained open wide and musical influences were left virtually unchecked. I must have taken full advantage of this freedom. After a concert in Munich, a film director I was friends with asked me whose band it was, mine or Jan's. Sometime later, after a short tour in Sweden, Jan asked to speak with me. Over coffee in a bistro we discussed the hierarchy in the band; Jan felt steamrolled by me. Our clear and open talk promptly put an end to my efforts to hog the limelight – and I kept a low profile from then on. I conceded that Jan had had good reason to put me in my place. I did not find it difficult not to have to stand in the front row all the time.

At this time Jan began to change his composition concept. Shortly after our talk, pieces emerged in his new programme in which the opportunities for outside influence were greatly reduced. Eternal jazz fans could protest now because jazz's inalienable freedom had been composed away – and they wouldn't be entirely wrong. Nonetheless, Jan's concept worked marvellously. This curtailed freedom made playing to the gallery much harder. The band became more "band-like," no longer a mere combination of individual performances. We were able to deal with this potential shortcoming because we all understood the new concept. Our aim was no longer: "Look at how great I am!" Instead, the band itself became our aim.

Opportunities for showmanship were now provided by the transitional solos, during which the rest of the band remained silent, giving top priority to the soloist. Once I got used to this, I missed nothing. Naturally, I can only speak for myself. It was almost liberating not having to assert oneself during the endless choruses. I have never been part of a more homogeneous band. I did everything to keep it that way, and enjoyed our joint success.

More and more, we set standards with the Jan Garbarek Group that are more commonly associated with classical music: getting onstage together in an orderly manner, bowing, focusing on the start without fiddling around with our instruments first. The concert would start with the first note. There was no warming up – this was to be done before the audience was admitted. After the last note faded away, we would present ourselves again, first standing, then bowing to give thanks for the applause. Die-hard jazz fans must have been in for a shock. Surely there had to be concertgoers who found our performances uptight or stuffy.

Yet I remain firmly convinced to the present day that the way we presented ourselves contributed significantly to our enormous success. The audience noticed that it was being taken seriously, and that the band took itself – and what it did – just as seriously. This never hurts – neither the musicians nor the listeners. After the last piece of the evening, we would bow again, and leave the stage together in an orderly fashion – well aware that this would not be possible without an encore. Now the audience had to do its part, earning the first encore with applause. A short while later, we were back, the applause even louder now, more grateful. A well-known, effective piece would be played, after which we disappeared backstage again. A longer wait this time. Then back onstage for a mellower piece, something to bring the evening to a close, to send everyone on their way. This is how the end of a show was normally scripted. Then, houselights! Meaning: the lights in the seating area would come up and the stage lights would be switched off.

Quite often, however, part of the audience refused to give up, while the rest were already moving towards the exits. It was relatively easy at this point to bring about grateful enthusiasm. All we had to do was wait one or two minutes longer, then switch the stage lights back on while simultaneously switching off the houselights. Back onstage! Hundreds of listeners would cheer, letting us know that they had won.

After that the audience would go home, content, and we would return to our hotel, acclaimed.

As a duo, Jan Garbarek and I had a few special experiences of our own. Now and then we would be invited to play in front of honoured guests. Once, this was on Petersberg, the mountain near Bonn, on the occasion of a state visit from the Norwegian royal couple. Pleasantries were exchanged at the subsequent reception and midday buffet. A few kind words were addressed to me. Jan, they'd already known personally for some time – he was a national hero in Norway. Rut Brandt, the wife of ex-chancellor Willy Brandt, also praised us for our performance, different as it was from the usual fare at state receptions.

It became even more obvious that our music was making inroads into traditionally classical terrain when Jan and I performed as a duo at a matinee organized on the occasion of the Goethe Prize awards ceremony in Munich's Herkules Hall. In the presence of then Federal President Richard von Weiszäcker and other honourable people, ambassadors of many countries, the function commenced with one of our duo pieces. As far as we were concerned, everything seemed to be taking its usual course. After the applause died down, we went backstage. There, we waited for our final performance to be announced.

While we were waiting, a department head of the Munich Headquarters excitedly joined us in the dressing room to tell us that the Head of the

Institute, Herr von Bismarck, had been so surprised and overwhelmed by our performance, that he had spontaneously changed his speech and mentioned us. After the festivities were over, we stood in the hotel lobby, waiting for the elevator. When we got in, it was full of high-ranking politicians, who proceeded to shower us with praise: "Quite extraordinary... Terrific!" By the door to the restaurant, Federal President von Weiszäcker was talking with the heads of the American and French embassies. We were intercepted outright: "Gentlemen, you are the heroes of the day!"

Von Weiszäcker added: "You have no idea how pleased I was not to have to listen to yet another string quartet."

The two ambassadors immediately wanted to know if we had released any records, and where they might be for sale...

Do I need to mention that this concluded our string of official invitations? In Germany jazz still isn't socially acceptable enough to exist in its own right alongside classical music. The chancellery isn't the White House. And it's much harder to picture Angela Merkel playing the saxophone than Bill Clinton.

I have always disliked the fact that my colleague Garbarek's saxophone playing keeps being referred to as "ice-cold." His clear, precise way of playing is responsible for this entirely inaccurate interpretation. This is aggravated by the fact that he is from the Far North, from Norway, near the Arctic. What doubts does this leave as to Jan's ice-cold sound? Just imagine Jan wasn't Norwegian, but Greek, and that his name was Garbaropoulos. All hell would break loose, and we would have to announce the saxophone's hottest sound – although it would be exactly the same. I, for my part, know a great number of saxophonists, and not one of them sounds as hot as Garbarek!

Initially I did not realize that my cooperation with Jan's band would turn into a sort of steady job. The fact that I didn't compose for the band didn't bother me. To the contrary – it allowed me to joke around with Jan: "So, have you written a new programme yet?"

After all, I knew I didn't have to put myself through this anymore. Neither of us is a prolific composer. We are jolly glad when a programme is completed. Neither I with Colours nor Jan with his Group ever changed a rehearsed, successful programme during its "run." Travelling and performing is more than enough to keep you busy. No need to add rehearsals for a new piece into the mix!

After twenty-five years, I was the most senior bandmember of the Garbarek Group. I probably would still be part of it today if it hadn't been for my stroke. During the initial time of uncertainty, when I still hoped for a full recovery, Jan kept assuring me that my place in the band was safe, that I could return immediately if fate restored my original faculties. Even my substitute, Juri Daniel, agreed – I was very touched. I had survived every single change in the band for over two decades. I was the only one who had never been replaced. Today, if anyone in the Garbarek Group misses me, it's only the older generation – the band has a new line-up. The process of forgetting often goes faster than one would like. But that, too, is part of life.

The Garbarekian quarter-century was a time in which I felt wholly fulfilled. After so many years spent in various kinds of bands, my urge to write for one had already been satisfied. My interest in a career of my own, on the other hand, is not something I had given up as a member in Jan's Group. Rather, I felt a continued interest in something of my own. Much as before, I was interested in sound, especially that of my own instrument. It's not as though I wanted to leave the band – I wanted to put ideas into practice that weren't necessarily part of the Garbarek Group's routine.

In the months we weren't on tour or in the studio, there was enough time to focus on my own stuff. I recorded solo albums, went on solo tours, and played as a guest with all sorts of musicians – and as a member of a very different ensemble.

15 United (Kingdom)

On tour in England with the United Jazz + Rock Ensemble: our tour schedule included Durham, a place that meant nothing to me back then. Although I hardly ever did any sightseeing when I was on tour, I'd noticed Durham's enormous cathedral during a short walk, and decided I wanted to have a closer look at the impressive structure. Once I got there, I noticed a plaque on one of the walls with a detailed account of how the cathedral had been "pieced together" over the centuries: construction had started in the Romanesque period, but the cathedral had then been perfected over time, piece by piece, from one end to the other, well into the Gothic age. As I stood there, reading the plaque, I heard sounds coming from somewhere and decided to follow them. On entering the edifice, I heard very interesting choral voices framed by a magnificent organ – a boys' and men's choir was rehearsing new choral music. No antiquated hymns, at last! Instead, rather peculiar harmonies. I had to listen to this, so I stayed. I remained in the cathedral for well over an hour, relishing the expansive acoustics with their monumental natural reverberation. The organ was fitted with pipes of a size I had not seen before. Rich low notes emerged from them – they must have had a diameter of at least one metre. I was "lost." This came as a surprise: I usually found sacred buildings to have more of a deterrent effect. Holy water, memorial candles and everlasting light aren't really my cup of tea.

But it was the music that guided me. Fascinated, I decided to return to the church the following morning to subject myself to the service before we continued our journey. The music made going inside the church possible– and so it happened. I arrived in time for the "performance." It started the way these things evidently always do: a little organ prelude, nothing out of the ordinary at first; then the bishop ascended the pulpit and theatrically delivered his incantatory sermon. At least, that's what it seemed like to me, listening to his beautiful English. I was willing to put up with this prologue – after all, I'd come for the music. Then, finally, it started: gloriously full and warm and modern, a little of each. The constant flow of latecomers was exasperating, though. Invariably, they let the heavy door slam shut behind them. Adding insult to injury, the gravel they unwittingly brought inside crunched with every step they took – terribly disruptive! It was no use, though. I had to put up with it: the stream of tourists was never-ending. Eventually, I stopped noticing. I was enthralled – the performance was reaching its climax.

Splendidly dressed servants of God walked down the central aisle to the impressive sound of the organ in what looked like extreme slow motion. Their power lay in their tempo. One has to have seen and heard this theatrical performance for oneself to be struck by it like I was. At night, I played hugely popular, well-received jazz rock with a band that set the house on fire. And the next morning I had my socks knocked off by sacred music that moved me to tears. What was wrong with me?

The United Jazz + Rock Ensemble had been founded in 1977. It was the brainchild of Werner Schretzmeier, the founder and director of Stuttgart's Theaterhaus. Back in the day he was an indefatigable driving force in Stuttgart and its surroundings – in fact, he still is. I'd met him in the 1960s, when he founded his political cabaret group *Die Widerständler*[1] and then Club Manufaktur in Schorndorf. For a while, there had even been talk of me getting involved in directing his cabaret ensemble. I can't remember why it came to nothing.

In the late 1960s, Werner boldly betook himself to television, where he was soon able to establish himself as a director of exciting, defiant youth programmes. In the mid-1970s, he planned the series *Goldener Sonntag*[2] for SDR, a show in real time in which a family would spend a Sunday morning together in front of the television while discussing the latest issues. The father was played by Hans-Dieter Hüsch, one of the daughters by Magdalena Thora, also known today as the jazz guitarist Leni Stern. A band would feature in each episode of this soap. Because of the youthful target audience, the music was meant to "rock" – so no "pure" jazz. Schretzmeier got in touch with Dauner, who in turn got in touch with his friends and acquaintances – this is how, after some time and several attempts, the permanent line-up of the United Jazz + Rock Ensemble came about, including ten musicians: Albert Mangelsdorff (trombone), Barbara Thompson and Charlie Mariano (both on the saxophone), Kenny Wheeler, Ian Carr and Ack van Rooyen (all on the trumpet), Volker Kriegel (guitar), Jon Hiseman on the drums, me on the bass, and, last but not least, Wolfgang Dauner on the piano. "The band of bandleaders" was its slogan – apart from a few little exceptions, it was true. At any rate, each and every one could have been a band leader.

1. The Resisters.
2. *Golden Sunday.*

Figure 30: Wolfgand Dauner, Eberhard Weber and Werner Schretzmeier (at the edge of the image), 1983

United became a success story. Our weekly television appearances quickly made the band famous across Germany, and we started playing together outside the TV studio, too. The band's appeal lay in its heterogeneity – from a musical point of view, we didn't fit together at all, but the friction created a special, unique sound which the public embraced. Once again, my theory was confirmed: the individual, the charismatic mattered more than sheer technical precision.

In fact, with our line-up, we wouldn't even have been capable of technical precision! I wasn't a jazz rock bass player, and very few producers would have thought of hiring Jon Hiseman for one of my recordings. Nonetheless, the success of the first LP, *Live im Schützenhaus*,[3] was extraordinary. In a short time, it became the most-sold German jazz record of all time, and the tours we were able to go on kept getting bigger.

It was fun to play with my old colleagues again. We all knew each other, but lately we'd only met at festivals where each of us was performing with their current band. Playing with United was very relaxing for me. The stress of leading your own band could really get to you. You had to be involved in everything: composing, arranging, tours, studios, marketing. At long last, I was just a sideman again.

Of course, the live recording made at the *Schützenhaus* had a few little glitches here and there. The perfectionists among us immediately started piping up, fighting for a follow-up LP carefully recorded in the studio. When it was released, it almost flopped. It didn't surprise me – the appeal of United lay in its diversity. We were no classical big band – the neat, the straight just wasn't our thing. United stood for the mix of individual artists that made it up; it wasn't a homogeneous orchestra. At any rate, I unequivocally pleaded for nothing but live recordings to be released from then on – and that is pretty much what happened.

Once, we gave a concert in Düsseldorf's Philipshalle. After the sound check, as we were waiting backstage for the concert to start, a pipe was being passed around – a popular pastime back then, not just in our band. I didn't see who among the wind players partook in the activity, but the rhythm group, Wolfgang Dauner, Volker Kriegel and I, certainly did. I think only Jon Hiseman showed any restraint. The marijuana had no effect on me initially – until the pipe was filled again and I inhaled deeply just before getting onstage. I'll never forget how bouncy the otherwise sturdy steps to the stage suddenly seemed. I managed to make it to my instrument more or less upright – the last hit had really got to me. Then the concert started.

There were various pieces in our programme which I had to give the cue for. My very first note was off. Sheer panic. How was this supposed to continue? Was I so stoned that the concert would have to be cancelled on my account? I regretted having taken that last hit, but there was no going back

3. *Live at the Marksmen's Clubhouse.*

now. I could only hope that the effects would eventually subside. But when would that be? There were horror stories about how long this sort of thing could last. We played the first piece. My error didn't seem to have been too serious. Suddenly, I was enjoying the drug! We played like devils, as if in a trance. Things were really taking off[4] (this was our favourite expression back then). I had totally lost track of time when Volker suddenly leaned over and yelled into my ear: "One!!" Evidently, the place I'd reached in the piece was completely different from where the rest of the band was. Somehow, I must have still followed the harmonies correctly. I'm acutely "allergic" to false notes and harmonies, and I simply cannot imagine having been so stoned that I suddenly would have tolerated them. I must have found the right place again because the rest of the piece went pretty well.

Figure 31: United Jazz + Rock Ensemble, from left to right: Ack van Rooyen, Kenny Wheeler, Wolfgang Dauner, Albert Mangelsdorff, Eberhard Weber, Charlie Mariano, Volker Kriegel, Ian Carr, Barbara Thompson and Jon Hiseman. Sheffield, UK, around 1984

Then, we started the second piece. Again, something was wrong with me. As soon as we finished playing the opening theme, the band stopped. The audience applauded as usual. What? No solos today? Why wasn't I aware of this? The effects of the pipe had hit me hard – I hadn't even noticed that all of the solos had already been played. It became frightfully clear to me that I might jeopardize the whole concert – I was experiencing severe memory

4. *Die Post ging ab.*

loss. What if it got even worse? Things somehow must have continued the way they were supposed to: I can't remember any other lapses. On the other hand, under these circumstances, I really wouldn't, would I? The first half was over, and by the time the second started, the effects of the pipe had subsided substantially. The cold sweat I'd broken out in may have helped flush out the toxins.

At the time of my first successes with Wolfgang Dauner, it was normal to try things out – the odd gateway drug or even stronger goodies once in a while. Once, in Frankfurt-Höchst, shortly before our trio was due to perform at a festival in the Centennial Hall, Wolfgang had appeared in my hotel room, saying, "Hey, I've got a few pills we could try!"

I was no advocate of the unknown – in fact, I tended to be rather scared of it. "What is it?"

"It's LSD."

They were small round blue pills, unremarkable, inoffensive-looking. Wolfgang had three, one for each of us in the trio. We'd heard a lot about the drug – several of these pills, it was said, would get you tripping. We all knew the stories of the poor souls that had jumped out the window after taking a few of these things, only to realize on awakening in hospital, if they were lucky, that human capacity for flight remains limited – even after the consumption of LSD.

Although we knew that we would be performing at the festival a few hours later, we decided to risk it. What harm could one little pill do? After all, a higher dose was needed for a real trip.

It's always exciting to take a new drug for the first time, not knowing what it will do to you. This one, though, didn't seem to be doing anything. At least, I didn't feel bad. Actually, something felt quite pleasant. Eventually, we had to go to the Centennial Hall. In the best of moods, we got into Wolfgang's car. Wolfgang tuned the radio to the AFN's[5] station. A military march was playing, the sort of thing that usually made me take flight. But this music was the best I had heard in a long time. We were in for an interesting evening…

Soon after we reached the hall, it was our turn, and we started doing our peculiar, free thing, using an old record player for the purpose, its sound scratchy and crackling. Nothing bothered us – we were perfect. At least, that's what it felt like to us. A very pleasant state in contrast to how spaced out the pipe in Düsseldorf had made me feel.

I was never granted the pleasure of repeating the experience – the little blue pills weren't easy to come by. I had to live with it. I wasn't ready to get into the business of procuring drugs. My duty to report the facts objectively demands that I point out that this was as illegal then as it is today. That didn't stop us from having a bit of fun every now and then.

5. The American Forces Network.

One thing I learned much later, long after joining the Jan Garbarek Group, is that I didn't need any drugs to almost ruin a concert. We'd just come back from a tour in the US, and right after that, we had another concert in Copenhagen, in a jazz club called the Montmartre. This is where our European tour was supposed to start. I volunteered to drive our van to Copenhagen. This was in the early days before we had roadies. Oddly enough I had no jetlag at all, feeling fresh and rested the whole drive. Just as well – it was a long way to Copenhagen. Once we got there, however, it was a different story. Minutes before our concert was due to start, the jetlag suddenly hit me – badly. I could hardly keep my eyes open. I was under the misguided impression that a big sip of white wine would quicken the spirit. It didn't – quite the opposite. How would I be able to stay awake? I had no choice. I had to get onstage!

As is known, I always sat on a stool to play. I cannot describe how I made it through the evening. I must have looked peculiar – my eyelids were at half-mast, at best. Shutting my eyes completely was impossible – I would have fallen into a deep sleep immediately, and, worse yet, I would have fallen off the stool with my bass. All I can recall is a dreadful evening and the constant fight not to fall asleep. During the break, a short nap backstage helped me get through the second half. It wasn't the first time I'd experienced that there are no quick fixes for jetlag. Only sleep. Definitely not alcohol or a hit from a pipe... My shock was so great that I never dared put myself in a similar situation again.

Figure 32: Wolfgang Dauner, Eberhard Weber, Volker Kriegel

A different, but equally unpleasant situation is when you notice as a passenger that the driver is fighting not to fall asleep, twitching and blinking every now and then, but still incapable of staying awake. I once went so far as to make a colleague drop me off at the nearest train station. He'd overexerted himself with his girlfriend the night before and was literally falling asleep at the wheel. My occasional screams were the only thing that got him to pay attention to the road. It's amazing how few accidents there are if you consider that bands are always on the road, driving from one concert to the next come rain or shine, in summer and in winter.

The relatively few accidents that did happen, though, are tragedies that etched themselves into my memory – nothing was ever the same again thereafter. One of my worst experiences was the tragic death of my friend and colleague Collin Walcott, the drummer of the band Oregon. In November 1984, on our way from Paris to Berlin, the Garbarek Group and I reached the site of a serious accident on the transit route through the GDR. We could still see debris scattered around the autobahn. It wasn't until we arrived in Berlin that we found out that just hours earlier Collin had died right there. Travelling in their big tour coach, Oregon had been involved in a terrible collision in the fog. Collin got stuck. The driver, injured himself, had managed to help Collin, but both died shortly thereafter. In a cruel twist of fate, Oregon had played at the same church we were headed to in Berlin for our concert that night.

What happened next with the United Jazz + Rock Ensemble? I toured with the band for twenty-five years until it split up in 2002. By then, we'd run out of steam. At some point, the tensions that had made up the band's sound turned into a burden – not uncommon after so many years spent working together. Under the circumstances, it was perfectly logical to take the appropriate next step. I left the band shortly before its breakup. The fans of precision in the band now had the opportunity to replace me with a bass guitar player. Tensions flared up, albeit for a short time only. I believe I'd felt the end coming sooner. There were personal reasons, too – but personal they shall remain.

In 2002 I was already on the road a lot with Jan Garbarek, so much so that it had become difficult to coordinate dates; leaving the Jazz + Rock Ensemble was easy under these circumstances. Besides, I didn't suffer from a want of variety. In 1982, on returning to my hotel in Hamburg from a rehearsal for my CD *Later That Evening* and another for a concert in the broadcasting hall of the Northern German Broadcasting Corporation (NDR), the receptionist handed me a note with a telephone number written on it: "A certain Frau Busch called while you were out."

Busch, Busch, a Frau Busch – who could that be? A number with the UK country code – 0044. Calling back didn't help – there was no answer. I had to wait until I returned home and mail from England landed in our letter box. Frau Busch turned out to be Kate Bush. We exchanged telephone numbers and were able to communicate verbally from then on. With neither the Internet nor mobile phones available back then, communication was often more complicated and protracted than it is today. Needless to say, I knew Kate as a popstar – after all, Maja, my wife, was a fan of hers and owned a few of her LPs. I knew of Kate's exceptional voice and talent for arrangements. Surprised that she knew my music and claimed to be a big fan of ECM, I became curious about her reason for contacting me. She then let the cat out of the bag and asked if I could fly to London to record a special bass melody which I was to think up for one of her tracks. Next, she sent me a tape – I can't recall the medium, probably a DAT. I thought of a few possibilities that matched her voice, scheduled a date for the recording and flew to London. When I arrived at the airport with all of my junk, she was there to pick me up in person with one of her brothers, and we drove to her flat. I'm not too clear on the details anymore, but I believe she was still living in some sort of flat share at the time.

The next day we went to the studio and I presented the melody I'd come up with. Kate sang to it and noticed that at one point her voice and my proposed melody got in each other's way. We were able to solve the problem, and the job was done.

A few years later, she called me again. This time, I didn't have to prepare anything in advance. I was flown in to record straight onto the tape. That, too, worked. Maja came with me this time. She and Kate had a lovely conversation in the evening. After that, we didn't see each other again for some time. Kate had a baby, little Albert. We eventually met again, on her gorgeous estate somewhere near Theale, where she was living with Albert and her husband Danny. It was an enormous property with a river running through it and an old mill with a functioning water wheel – very romantic. I was given an apartment of my own in the main building. A cook had been hired for the occasion – I ate very well. The recordings were made in her own studio, at a short distance from the main building, in converted garages. This was at a time when I was in a position to make many suggestions as a contribution to her half-finished songs. Kate shared the well-known tendency of pop producers to "decide later on." Weeks later, long after I'd returned home, I was finally able to listen to the sample copy and find out which of my versions had been chosen and which hadn't.

Back then Kate had already retreated from the concert business – she still produced LPs, but no longer performed in public. During one of our cosy evenings together, over a wonderful meal accompanied by several glasses of red wine, Kate hinted at the fact that if she was ever to give concerts again, she would want me to be there. When I found out in the summer of 2014 that the time had finally come, and Kate was going to get back onstage for the first time in thirty-five years, my phone didn't ring – I had told her long ago that my musical career had been cut short. Instead, I later received an email from her. What she wrote moved me: "Did I tell you that we played your stunning Pendulum CD in the venue before each and every show as it's my very favourite album!"

Figure 33: Eberhard Weber and Kate Bush in the London studio around 1982/83. The photo was used for Kate's CD *Director's Cut*.

So I had been there all the same!

Right from the start I have found Kate to be a truly endearing person, warm-hearted, generous and humble. Even if I wanted to, I wouldn't be able to think of anything negative to say about her. My detractors will be shocked: Weber, the eternal critic, is full of praise! She reacted splendidly to my strokes of fate – my stroke in 2007 and the sudden, unexpected death of my wife Maja in 2011. An admirable, exceptional woman.

16 Border Crossings

When I think about the time before I became a pro, I remember imagining that all any musician ever thought about was music. I never bothered thinking about what goes on backstage, let alone what a band does all day. I didn't find out until later that the effect these things can have on the everyday life of a professional is far from negligible. I have met celebrated ensembles that spent weeks on tour without exchanging a single word; in the evenings, the audience would have no idea. This is how it should be, but it also goes to show that on a daily basis, strictly musical problems are often far from being the biggest problems to overcome on tour. At times it is little short of a miracle that anything acceptable can be performed at all – a friend is seriously ill, you are having personal problems. Or you "only" have a cold to get over. Leave your colleagues high and dry? Disappoint the audience and let the event organizers deal with the losses? Unthinkable! In South America we had terrible diarrhoea, in South Korea we played in an unheated hall – in winter! The audience sat bundled up in thick coats, hats and blankets; our hands were ice-cold. Playing without gloves was unthinkable – on the other hand, so was playing with gloves. In Hungary, we had the opposite problem in summer. Without air conditioning, temperatures in the sports hall we were performing in reached those you would expect in a sauna. After the concert, when we reached the dressing room, we looked as though we'd showered in our suits: sopping wet and soggy, sweat stinging our eyes.

With all the travelling I was doing, I often crossed paths with my colleagues; time after time we would meet at one airport or another. The most surprising thing would have been not to run into anyone. On one Berlin flight, I noticed the conductor Sir Georg Solti, famous the world over, sitting in economy class – oddly enough – just a few rows ahead of me, to the left. During the entire flight, the maestro flipped through his score, conducting. All I could see was the back of his head and his right arm waving around. He must have been totally lost in thought. When the "prepare for landing" announcement was made, he just continued conducting. Even after we had landed, when all the other passengers got up and started pressing towards the exits, Solti remained in his seat, studying the score. As I passed his row, I peeked at it. The partition was covered with signs and notations in many different colours. I was impressed – had I not been, I would have forgotten the incident long ago.

A musician's trips are no different from anyone else's, except for the fact that musicians tend to travel much more often than people with other jobs. In fact, we spend most of our time on the road, at airports or in the air. Compared to this, the amount of time we spend onstage is almost marginal. For those who travel only three or four times a year, the problems associated with it can even be part of the fun. They stop being fun, though, when you have to make it to a concert on time.

Towards the end of my career, I no longer enjoyed going on tour and having to perform night after night. It was a never-ending cycle of driving or flying hundreds of kilometres, checking in at hotels, eating generally mediocre food, waiting in hotel rooms, doing sound checks in cold halls and waiting some more for concerts to start. Then back to the hotel and on to the next city the next day. A different hotel every night, no sightseeing, no fun. Hitting the pavement isn't compatible with performing at night. I'd been to Rome five times and never seen the sights. I knew the airport, the hotels and the venues. It wasn't until the sixth time that I asked the taxi driver to swing by the Colosseum, so that I, too, could say I'd "been to" Rome. The Vatican, too, I only ever got to see from afar.

I'd like to share with you what happens when the customs office gets involved. I think it used to be even worse. Then a jolt went through Germany, and many of these bureaucratic institutions suddenly became friendlier – often even pleasant. Who among members of my generation can't remember that the mail used to be state-run, that in post offices only one in eight counters would be open, while the other seven workers would stand around in the background, chatting in plain sight, loath to deal with tedious customers. This changed at some point. Government offices turned into citizen offices – were we not citizens before that? I have nothing against this, though, if things stay this way. I can't judge what customs is like today, but back in my day, you needed a so-called carnet to cross a border with your equipment and avoid paying duty on your instruments and accessories. This sounds logical, simple even, at first. You begin by going to the Chamber of Commerce and Industry, called CCI, to collect a form on which you list the goods you intend to take out of the country. These are goods you have no intention of selling abroad and which you want to bring back in their entirety. Once this form is filled in, it has to be returned to the CCI. There, it must remain – pay close attention – for twenty-four hours before it is stamped, and you can collect it. Only then can you contact customs. The reasoning behind this remains a mystery to me to this day.

In Munich, I thus loaded my car with my various cases and drove to the customs office, where I presented my form from the CCI to a customs officer, who checked it carefully. "What is this?"

"Accessories, like spare parts, for example!"

"There's a separate form for accessories. Fill it in and come back when you are done!"

I sat at a desk and spent what must have been a solid half hour listing every little cable and battery I was travelling with. When I returned to the counter, the officer was nowhere to be seen. Was he on his break? Was he done for the day? As I stood there looking clueless, another officer noticed me: "What are you looking for?"

"Your colleague."

"He isn't here. Can I help you?"

I got excited – he wanted to help! I handed over my freshly filled-in form and the spare parts.

"What is this?"

"Accessories, like spare parts, for example!"

"Nonsense! These are spare and wear parts. There's no need…!"

"I'm sorry, but your colleague…"

He crossed out the list.

"And where are the goods?"

"Outside, in the car!"

He stamped my form and handed it to a colleague: "Go outside with the gentleman and have a look at the goods."

This didn't bode well. I could already picture myself lifting all the heavy cases out of the car. Outside, the officer just looked through the back window of my vehicle and asked: "Are these the instruments?"

My nodding was enough to satisfy him. The inspection was over, and he returned the stamped papers to me. "Have a good trip!"

I had everything I needed to legally cross borders.

There is one truly remarkable trip with the Jan Garbarek Group that I remember on account of the hassle with customs alone. Each of us made his own way to the West Coast of the USA with all his gear. From there, the tour was supposed to take us north, to Canada. We all had had enough experience of carnets by then to decide for ourselves whether we wanted to go through the rigmarole again or just hope for charitable officers instead. They did exist: "I'll let it pass this time, but next time…"

I decided to take the risk: I'd got lucky several times before. My flight left from Munich, where none of the customs officers showed any interest in my suitcases and cases. On my way to Los Angeles, I had to change flights in Chicago, and thus go through customs there because my next flight was domestic. I wheeled my carefully stacked suitcase and cases, all four of them, towards the customs area. In front of me, other passengers with both small and large suitcases were already waiting for instructions from a heavy-set female officer who directed them in one direction or another. Then it was my turn. I had far more luggage than anyone else. She indicated that I should go all the way to the right. I saw a door made of frosted glass and immediately thought to myself, "special treatment." That's all I needed! I didn't have a carnet on me... I pushed my wobbly "vehicle" towards the door and stuffed it through, into a dark corridor. At the other end there was a second door, also made of frosted glass. I kept going, pushed it open – and ended up in the arrivals hall! How could this be? I'd entered the USA without being inspected!

I then caught my flight to Los Angeles. No customs again. Hurrah! The tour could begin – for me. Things didn't look as good for Jan. He'd chosen the tedious carnet option and procured all the necessary exit stamps for his two pieces of luggage: a saxophone case and a heavy case full of reverberators and effects processors. On arriving in Los Angeles, he promptly obtained the required entry stamp. Easy. From then on, however, every border crossing turned into an ordeal for him. "Where is the customs area?" he would ask.

"Only in the arrivals hall!"

"You've got to be kidding!"

The following journey, to Canada this time, was unusual in that a ferry took us to Victoria. Jan had to insist on his carnet stamps again. Once more, we asked: "Which way to customs?"

The ferry staff informed us: "There's no more customs area here!"

But Jan was deeply committed to the Norwegian customs office: "I need a stamp!"

More shrugging – but this time, it was accompanied by a useful hint: "The old customs barrack is over there. Maybe you'll find an old stamp lying around!"

Evidently, Michael DiPasqua was still harbouring traces of the American pioneering spirit: "I'll go check!"

Oddly enough, even though the customs office was "out of business," the door wasn't locked. After no more than a few minutes, Mike reappeared with both a stamp and an ink pad. Splendid! Now Jan would be able to travel to Canada with us. After performing the bureaucratic act, Mike wanted to return the stamp and ink pad to the barrack. This time, however, the door wouldn't open. After a brief discussion, we agreed on the most mundane of solutions: we left the stamp and the inkpad under the doormat. We are not in a position to give information about any further developments.

This memorable journey through North America ended with a final customs incident in New York. Again, Jan Garbarek was the whipping boy. The rest of us were already on our way home: DiPasqua stayed in the States, and Rainer and I flew to Germany. Having stayed in New York for accounting purposes, around four o'clock in the afternoon Jan headed to JFK airport with his two items of goods subject to customs control. He went straight to the SAS Scandinavian Airlines terminal to catch the eight o'clock flight to Oslo that evening: "Can I leave my cases here? I still need my exit stamp."

Figure 34: Michael DiPasqua, Eberhard Weber, Jan Garbarek, David Torn

"Ikke noe problem."

Which meant: "No problem." Here, too, however, the customs area could only be found in the arrivals terminal. Getting there involved a trip in the shuttle-bus, which takes a solid half hour at JFK airport. On arrival, he was faced with New York's strict conditions: prohibited access to the customs area. Jan tried to sneak through the sliding doors activated by arriving passengers headed in the opposite direction. Stop! More New York conditions, this time in the shape of security personnel: "What are you looking for?"

"Customs."

Jan was handed a large sign he had to hang around his neck so he could move around in the customs area unhindered – until the customs officer gave him the next fright: "Where are the goods?"

"Over at SAS!"

"Bring them over!"

Shuttle back to SAS. Jan knew there was no way he'd be able to transport his cases without assistance. A porter would have to help him. Locating one isn't a problem at an airport like JFK. But not one was willing to accompany Jan and his cases to the customs area. Why? It was five o'clock. "It's rush-hour. I can't waste a whole hour on a single passenger!"

Can you believe it? Jan had to call a haulier in the city to book a vehicle that would transport the two cases to customs, where a different officer – the first one was off duty by now – stamped Jan's carnet without so much as looking at the goods. After the last call – the very last call – to passengers boarding the flight to Oslo, Jan made it onboard after four whole hours of bureaucratic frustration!

When I think about concerts and events that took place in the last forty years, incidents like this one inevitably resurface. It's hard to believe, but I have no other memories of this tour in the States and Canada. Probably the tour was a success, maybe even worth reporting about. I still can't remember anything about Canada, not even the names of the cities we played in, except for Toronto. But only because that is from where we flew back to the States, so we must have played there the night before.

17 Highs and Lows

Music doesn't always come first during a tour. The culinary offerings rank pretty high for many jazz musicians. On one occasion, we were giving a concert for Hartmann, a company producing medical devices, at their plant in Heidenheim, in Swabia. As usual, there was catering backstage organized by our management with a special request for local specialties, so that at least our diet would be somewhat varied.

Over to the expert now, the Swabian *Maultaschen*[1] lover: to this day I have never tasted better *Maultaschen*. They were so good, it's a miracle I was even capable of playing decently.

Whether warm sausages really have a place in the culinary pantheon is debated among gourmets. I, for one, remember two jazz clubs whose yearly bookings I always accepted gladly on account of the giant sausages served there with hot mustard during the breaks. These clubs mustn't remain in the shadows. One was the Domicile in Munich before it moved from Siegesstrasse to Leopoldstrasse. After the move, it lost much of its original character because the owner decided to run the club according to the American model. This meant changing programmes every week. Munich isn't New York, so by 1981 the Domicile's days in the Bavarian capital were over.

The other club was the Ulmenwall Bunker in Bielefeld, run by a young married couple. Later, when the lease was regrettably transferred to new personnel, the extraordinary sausages were replaced by a "normal" brand. From then on, jazz musicians only drove to the Bunker for the music.

I have to admit that another thing I've always enjoyed is collecting negative examples: the worst hotels, the lousiest restaurants. I will stick to one guesthouse and a few hotels here.

In Vienna: the edges of the lino squares are peeling off, turning them into trip hazards. The "toilet" is a hole in the floor in the middle of the room

---

1. Swabian Maultaschen, literally "mouth pockets," are similar to ravioli, but larger in size.

– mind you, you can draw a curtain round it. I am on tour with the guitarist Bill Frisell. We agree that the first one of us to wake up will knock on the other's door. Then we'll make our escape. Breakfast on the autobahn can only be better.

In Algiers: the bathtub is full of excrement. The previous occupant used it as a toilet.

In Poona: countless cockroaches. The toilet in the room is in plain sight, offering no privacy. Or a flush... Ralf Hübner, the drummer, keeps the light on all night because he heard that it keeps the roaches away.

In Vancouver: the bathroom is filthy. The floor is so sticky our shoes stick to the tiles. There are rotting vegetables in the fridge.

In Stuttgart: the bathroom is unusable. There is a bathtub and a sink. So far so good. There are two taps for the bathtub – one for hot water, the other for cold water. But the faucet handle for the cold water is missing. The hot water is scalding, and thus unusable. For the sink, there is a mixer tap. When you turn it on, a single jet of water spurts out horizontally over the lip of the sink, right onto your body.

For the hotel in Edinburgh, I have to give more context. Rarely have I been as cold as in Great Britain. Winter in British hotels had to be taken literally, at least in the 1970s and '80s. Hard to imagine for continentals: even luxurious establishments skimped on the heating. Only the "normal" businessman mattered to establishments such as these: he went to sleep around ten, got up at seven, left the building and returned around six in the evening. This meant that from ten at night to six in the morning and from nine in the morning to six in the evening the heating was off. The daily and nightly routine of musicians, however, is incompatible with these cost-cutting measures. Too bad if you had to stay at a hotel like this for more than a day. By the time you got back to your room from a concert, around midnight, it was already freezing. We were freezing. When you returned to your room after breakfast, around nine, the cold was already sneaking up on you. The rooms then remained unheated until six o'clock in the evening. We were miserably cold all day. When the heat finally got turned on, we were already on our way to the sound check in an equally cold and draughty hall in which the heating had been off all day. Back in our rooms around midnight, we found them to be bloody cold again. To make matters worse, a wretched draught seeped through the poorly sealed single-glazed windows.

Back to the aforementioned hotel in Edinburgh: it was winter, again. I arrived at the hotel and went to my room. It was tiny. Where was the heater? I looked everywhere: behind the curtains, in the corners. Nothing! Back to the front desk. There, I was given an astonishing explanation: "This room is so small that it doesn't need a heater. It's heated by the neighbouring rooms – the walls are really thin."

Even more astonishing: it was true! The Scottish room really was warm enough at night.

I do have good memories, however, of British gastronomy – memories that verge on being moving. Once, on my way to Scotland with the Garbarek Group, around lunchtime we decided to follow a sign to a pub. The old building it was located in was pleasant, British, quaint, and "in the middle of nowhere." We liked it. When we entered, just like everywhere else, it was cold. The young publican rushed over immediately to get a fire going in the open fireplace. It really did get warm, especially if you sat close to it. We were the only customers. Something quite pleasant, something jazzy, was playing in the background. When we told the publican that we liked the music – he turned out to be a jazz fan and a connoisseur – he put on his favourite records. Happy and contented in this congenial atmosphere, we placed our order. The publican was also our chef and waiter. Everything was very peaceful and pleasant, and we asked our host to sit with us. He told us that he rarely had the opportunity to go to a jazz concert in Edinburgh. He was sorry to have missed Charlie Mariano, who had appeared there with this German bass player, Eberhard Weber. We smiled, but didn't tell him who we were. Evidently, he didn't recognize us – he couldn't believe it when our British tour escort spilled the beans as we were leaving: "This is Eberhard Weber!"

We almost felt sorry for our host – he was so embarrassed he hadn't recognized me. Stunning him a second time, our road manager added: "And this is Jan Garbarek!"

18 To Poona, Please!

How many trips have I been on and how many concerts have I played in forty years? I once tried adding them all up and reached a total of several years spent onstage without a single break, night after night – be it in Esslingen's Jazzkeller or any of the other smoke-filled dens of Villingen, Stuttgart, Hamburg, Munich, Hannover, Bielefeld or elsewhere. People still chain-smoked back then, ruining their own health and that of others – without realizing it. The air quality only improved gradually, when the venues we played in during our early years no longer measured up to the growing interest and audiences we were generating, and concert halls started opening their doors to us. Those who begrudged us our success would comment, "Too good for the cellars now, are you?"

I never stopped performing in jazz clubs! By now they, too, are smoke-free. Even so: What is so reprehensible about enjoying performing in venues that are well cared for? About not being woken up in the morning by the smell of smoke and mildew wafting over from the clothes you wore the night before? On top of this, demand for the limited number of seats available "underground" simply became too big. We – both Colours and the Jan Garbarek Group later on – gladly took on the challenge.

As a jazz musician of a certain stature, you really do get around! Where haven't I been! It's easier to list the places I haven't been to.

In Europe, it's simple: there's only Andorra and Monte-Carlo. And Greenland.

In South America: Tierra del Fuego and Ecuador.

In Asia: Burma (Myanmar today), Vietnam, North Korea and China.

North America: there is no country I haven't been to.

That leaves only the North Pole. The South Pole is missing, too, but parts of it are claimed by Australia, where we brought joy to two Tasmanian cities: Hobart and Launceston.

Africa, with its new states, would be worth a go, too. So far, I've made it as far as Sudan.

On our way to Sri Lanka, or Ceylon, as it was known back then, we once had a layover in Singapore, but only to spend the night. We had hardly arrived when we were confronted by the tyranny typical of the times: Singapore did not let men with long hair into the country. Your hair couldn't touch your collar or your ears. Endless palaver with the customs officers. There was chopped-off hair all over the floor: many a hippie had given in.

With the three of us – Jasper van't Hof, Ralf Hübner and me – there wasn't a chance we would let anyone cut our hair. What was to be done? Eventually, two seats were found on a flight leaving for Ceylon immediately. But there were three of us. I offered to stay behind, and spent the night in the transit area, sleeping on a leather bench. At some point, all the lights were switched off, and it got quiet. For the rest of the night, though, every hour or so the roller shutters of the shop and boutique fronts would be drawn up and the lights turned on again – a sure sign that a plane was arriving for a stopover. A great hullaballoo would ensue – until the plane took off again and darkness returned to the transit area.

Musicians are long-distance drivers, frequent flyers, professional travellers. The time we spend onstage is a fraction of the time we spend on the road. I owe my most dramatic journey to an invitation from the Goethe Institute, when I was asked to put together a band for a tour of Asia. I insisted on having Jan Garbarek join me. At the time he hadn't been to Asia, and I was already playing in his band, the Jan Garbarek Group. I hired Ralf Hübner as a drummer – he'd already been on countless Asian tours. I also engaged a young newcomer as the keyboarder. This tour turned into an existential experience for me – I could write a whole book about it. Here, however, I only want to mention one episode. It begins with the head of the local Goethe Institute in Lahore, Pakistan oversleeping – right at the start of the tour. The morning after our first concert, he was supposed to drive us to the airport so that we could fly on to Poona via Bombay, or Mumbai, as it is called today. Because he overslept, though, this did not happen. Without his assistance, we still managed to get to the airport with all our gear an hour before our flight's scheduled departure. Surprised and relieved, we noticed that the departures hall was virtually empty: great, we'd made it! We started piling up our cases and suitcases in front of the airline's check-in counter. Then, nothing happened for a long time. While we were waiting, the Goethe man arrived at the airport, apologizing profusely. Familiar with the local conditions, he dreaded the worst. Frantically, he started running around, making enquiries while we watched our luggage. When he returned, he was white as a sheet. "Too late! Check-in is over. The gate is closed!"

No wonder the hall was empty. His failure to wake up on time that morning triggered a disastrous chain-reaction: back then, flights in Asia were generally booked out weeks in advance. It looked as though we were going to have to stay put for quite some time! Basically, all our other concerts in India, Thailand, Indonesia, Malaysia and Japan were on the line. In a state of sheer panic, the Goethe man bid us goodbye and raced to his office to inform the other organizers and save what could be saved. To make matters worse, it was Sunday!

Not knowing what to do, the four of us sat on our luggage in the empty hall and waited. Now and then a door would open, and airline staff would write something incomprehensible to us on a blackboard in Hindi or Urdu. Occasionally, I would ask one of them if there were any flights that we might be able to get on. Nothing could be done. We waited some more.

Then a door opened and a man in a Pakistan Airlines uniform came into the hall. I approached him immediately. "We are German musicians and we are stuck. Can you help us?"

He looked sceptical, but something had caught his attention. It soon became clear what: "German" was the key word. He told me that he liked Germans, and that his brother was the manager of the Ramada Hotel in Frankfurt. As chance would have it, I had stayed at the very same hotel with United just a few days earlier. I had noticed the interesting name of the "manager on duty" on a sign at reception – an unusual, Asian-sounding name. Capitalizing on this coincidence, I told the airline employee about it, embellishing the story somewhat by saying, not quite truthfully, that I had met his brother. The ice was broken. He immediately asked me to join him in his office. He sat down in front of his computer – and summarily kicked four passengers off the next flight out. It was going to Karachi. He printed our boarding passes and told a porter to put our cases and suitcases into a large container, so that our luggage could be loaded onto the plane at once. The problem was solved. For now.

In Karachi, too, the flights to Poona were all full. But here, the local head of the Goethe Institute was able to help. His Pakistani secretary knew a Pakistan Airlines employee who followed the example of his colleague in Lahore, and struck four names off the list of passengers to Bombay. It still wasn't Poona, but at least we were making some progress.

We were bothered by the way connections and corruption determined everyday life here as a matter of course. Yet at the same time, at that moment, we were glad about it – we might still be on a waiting list today had things been any different.

In Bombay, we were faced with the now familiar question of how to continue our journey. We had no contacts at the Goethe Institute here, although we did at the German consulate. So we called. While this is easy enough today, back then it involved "queuing up" until a telephone set became available. Queueing was an unknown concept. There was no helping it: consideration for others gave way to jostling, sharp elbows and chaos. I first had to get used to this – I was surprised the other jostlers made way when I joined in the fray. When I called the German consulate, I was told that on account of then Minister President of Baden-Württemberg Lothar Späth's visit, no one would be available to assist us. Politics before culture. I summoned all my powers of persuasion. At least I managed to get one consular official to meet us at the airport and help us think about our options. The civil servant made the compelling suggestion that, since he wasn't in any position to get us onto a continuing flight, we travel to Poona by land, a journey shorter than the one from Frankfurt to Cologne or from Munich to Stuttgart. No problem! Of course, we could cover the distance by car. A taxi for three people and a cargo taxi for all our equipment and the fourth man – that could work. From a European perspective, at least. I was the band leader, so I would travel with the equipment – that went without saying. I also had dollars in my pocket to deal with any tolls we might encounter on the way. My colleagues were to follow in the taxi.

The lorry arrived first, a vehicle I have trouble describing. Inoperative by German standards, it would be considered a wreck in our part of the world. Actually, I would go one step further: back home, this vehicle would be taken off the streets immediately.

Two young drivers were sitting in the lorry. Due to its front-mid-engine layout, there were only two seats in the cabin. The driver sat behind the steering wheel on the right, and I in the passenger seat to his left – India has left-hand traffic. Somehow the second driver managed to squat on the engine's metal cover. I have no idea how hot the metal got. The music instruments had been stowed away in the back under my colleague's watchful eye. Off we went.

Bombay's airport is by the sea, and to get to the mainland to reach Poona, a long stone bridge had to be crossed. I soon realized that our drive was going to be an experience. This realization, in turn, gave way to the fear that it may be my last.

There was construction on the bridge. I noticed with horror that there was only one lane – the second was torn up. Far below us, you could see the sea. For a European, it was inconceivable that cars were allowed on the bridge under these circumstances – without any safety measures. On top of that, I had no idea that in India there was no such thing as turn-taking, with traffic in opposing directions taking turns to use a single lane, the whole thing neatly choreographed by traffic lights.

Instead, traffic going in both directions now simultaneously converged in the same lane. Was this really happening? First, vehicles drove towards each other. Then they tried to inch past each other – it was more a question of millimetres! The whole episode was accompanied by endless palaver and arguments, with everyone involved fighting to get ahead. I could see that in some cases, only one half of a tyre was actually on the road, while the other was spinning mid-air, with nothing but the sea below. I had no choice but to leave it to fate and put my faith in the skills of the young Indian driver at the wheel. It took many endless minutes until, incredibly, the lorry reached the mainland. All clear! We soon came across road signs with Hindi letters on them, which neither of the two drivers apparently knew what to do with – they stopped at each one, holding lengthy discussions.

Towards evening we reached a steep pass. Were we going to climb it in this vehicle? I hadn't realized that Poona lies at a much higher altitude than Bombay. We started our ascent. It turned out that our horn wasn't working. While this may not be a big deal for non-Indians, in India the horn is vital. Cutting corners would be unavoidable on this narrow pass. Honking indicated that there was oncoming traffic. According to Indian logic, no honking back meant that no one was driving towards you. If this was the case, you drove fast and fearlessly, even if there was a hairpin bend ahead. As we had no horn, however, we couldn't play by these rules.

As night fell, we continued pushing upward. More and more lorries occupied the road. Smoke and the unbearable stench of exhaust fumes made it increasingly hard to breathe. I used my scarf as a filter to protect myself from the black wads of smoke. In the fading light of day I could make out lorries that had crashed into the abyss, their wheels pointing skywards. Were they still turning? My initial fear gradually turned into full-fledged horror.

As the winding road became steeper, the behemoths on it grew slower, forming an unending column. Smoking and stinking, they laboured upwards. Unfortunately, my drivers knew nothing about changing gears: even though our vehicle was getting slower and slower, they tried to master the incline in fourth gear. Neither of them spoke a word of English, so I tried to convey by all means possible – signing and gesticulating – that it would be advisable to switch to a lower gear. It was pointless. In the looming darkness, we continued creeping upwards – the pointer on the dial of the oil pressure gauge moving closer towards the red zone with every metre we gained in altitude. Eventually, as was to be expected, the engine died: it was over. We'd just reached a hairpin bend, an endless line of vehicles in our wake.

The two colleagues sat in the cabin discussing what was to be done. I noticed that the driver doggedly kept his foot on the brake. Only then did I realize that the handbrake was faulty, too – on a steep mountain pass with a bottomless abyss. At some point the second driver, who had been squatting on the hot engine cover until then, slid over to the right side to help his colleague. He took control of the brake pedal, so that the first driver could view the damage from outside. Our situation couldn't have been all that unusual, considering that I saw him grab a wedge, presumably to jam it under the tyres. He then signalled to the second driver that he could slowly back down towards a tree – that was standing on the edge of a precipice! All of this took place in total darkness and without reversing lights. It was madness.

At least, two safeguards had now been found: the wedge and the tree. My misgivings prompted me to try and get out of the lorry, but the door handle was missing on the passenger side. The door was wired shut. I threw myself against it, but my panic-fuelled attempts to open it failed. I was trapped, at night, in the middle of nowhere in India, without a phone, totally helpless. Eventually, our lorry seemed somewhat secure – in a bend on the brink of an abyss.

More palaver between the drivers. I got the impression that they were seriously considering turning around somehow in order to let the lorry roll down the pass and drive back to Bombay. Even if that had worked, what was I supposed to do in Bombay? I felt another surge of panic. I imagined the worst: they would take my dollars, abandon me and leave with all of the instruments. Not a bad deal for a couple of poor Indians.

I prayed that the stalled engine would recover, that we would be able to keep creeping up that pass – it couldn't be much further to the summit.

Suddenly I saw in the faint moonlight that a black monstrosity was reversing down the pass towards us – some sort of lorry. What was going on now? It was a tow truck! There was hope again. A massive iron chain was attached to our front axle, and with a frightfully violent jolt, we were pulled off the wedge, away from the tree. Through some sort of miracle, our axle wasn't yanked off. The driver got back into the cabin and, slowly, we were dragged up the pass. Surely, we would reach the top at any moment now. But no – the tow truck turned left onto a sort of parking lot and left us there. I finally managed to push open my door and got out. There I was now, somewhere in India, in the middle of the night, as helpless as I had ever been.

When I later thought about how it was possible for a tow truck to show up out of the blue in the middle of nowhere, I was able to find only one explanation: since breakdowns of this sort were the norm, this is exactly what the business must have specialized in. If that was the case, it was also normal that they should charge a fee for their service. Not in Indian rupees, however – only in hard currency. As far as foreigners were concerned, at any rate.

My long blond hair made it hard for me to pass as Indian. I can't remember how the driver of the tow truck conveyed the amount or the currency to me. I unpacked my US dollars. I have to admit that I'd love to know today how much I paid him – was it ten dollars? Twenty? Fifty? More? It's quite possible that, shocked as I was, I presented him with a range of banknotes and let him choose.

While we were sitting tight in the parking lot, and the endless column of lorries and cars kept moving past us, I suddenly heard my name being called: "Eberhard!"

How was this possible? Who – besides my colleagues – would be calling my name in the middle of the night here in India? I was saved! Which of the vehicles in this never-ending line were they sitting in? The column inexorably moved on. So much for being rescued! No one was stopping. I stayed behind in the darkness.

More waiting. Waiting. What for? Eventually another miracle took place: the driver was able to restart the engine! We clambered in and continued our upward journey in the wrong gear. It didn't take long for the dial of the oil pressure gauge to move towards the red zone again. But we made it. As dramatic as it may sound: with a final jolt, we reached the top of the pass. Here, we found a house and, most importantly, water to fill our empty radiator. It seemed to me that litres on litres of water were poured in, enough to fill a whole bathtub.

The last part won't take long to tell. We arrived safely in Poona, where my colleagues were already waiting for me at the home of the local Goethe Institute's head. Only now did they find out how catastrophic my journey had been. When they'd called my name near the mountain-pass parking lot – it had been them! – they thought that the two drivers and I were just taking a break. They went on to tell me about their taxi-driver's adventurous manoeuvres. But there was no doubt that my experience took the biscuit.

Figure 35: Eberhard Weber and Jan Garbarek in the sports hall in Neuwied during rehearsals for the planned Asian tour, around 1986

Obviously, when concertgoers settle into their seats, full of anticipation for the performance about to begin, they don't think of what might crop up when musicians go on tour – even if it isn't always quite so dramatic. How could listeners possibly imagine what it sometimes takes to guarantee their enjoyment? How could they know that it's sometimes necessary to weigh the odds of whether an event should take place at all? Like, for example, when your fees barely cover the excess baggage on a flight – which happens more often than you'd think. Should you play for free that night? Will a second, better-paid concert make up for it? For a while, my colleagues and I knew an employee of SAS Scandinavian Airlines, a jazz fan, who did his best again and again to spare us any excess baggage fees. He helped us whenever possible, which is why we frequently flew via Copenhagen, the SAS hub. It was actually cheaper for us to fly from Munich to Budapest via Copenhagen without excess baggage fees than straight from Munich to Budapest with thousands of euros to cough up for our luggage. Our benefactor operated according to the principle that business class passengers generally travelled with nothing but their carry-on luggage, not using their free thirty-kilo allowance. This meant that ten business people made 300 kilos of free baggage available to us (in theory). Unfortunately, not all section heads at SAS saw it like that.

By the way, my Indian pass adventure took place on 22 January, my birthday. That night I celebrated it as if I'd been reborn. My two drivers drove back to Mumbai the same night. I have no idea if they ever made it back or if they still provide their services with the same vehicle today.

19 Home Advantage?

As exhausting as all this travelling around is, jazz musicians can't escape it. Just like football teams, some feel much better playing at home. Others, however, can't do so without frayed nerves.

It doesn't seem to make any difference whether you've already travelled halfway around the world, scoring triumph after triumph. When you get close to your hometown, it's as if New York, San Francisco, Rome, Buenos Aires, Tokyo and Sydney don't matter anymore. Very odd! I would have expected the opposite to be true: nervous in the metropolises, relaxed at home. Rarely have I been as tense and anxious as the night I had a solo scheduled in my hometown's tiny club, the Jazzkeller, in Esslingen am Neckar. I had just returned from a triumphant concert in London – and barely managed to string together anything decent in Esslingen. Annoyingly odd, oddly annoying. Many of my colleagues feel the same way: Jan Garbarek in Oslo, Rainer Brüninghaus in Cologne, my American colleagues from New York. Never have I heard Bill Frisell and Michael DiPasqua as helpless as the time we played in one of New York's famous jazz clubs. It's tempting to ban home concerts. Anywhere but home.

20 Perfect Sound

At a certain age, I started asking myself two questions. First, what was my best concert? And second, what was the worst of my career? Instantly, you run into the problem of what "good" and "bad" actually mean. And who determines this? What are the criteria? Success with the audience, applause? Or is it something more technical: the sound? The sound where: onstage or in the hall? And where in the hall: up above, down below, in the middle, in the back or on the side? As musicians, we only ever receive this information after a concert – from the organizer, from critics, from audience members who approach us. Or from our own crew. They, however, will be wary of calling the sound bad. Thus we never really know what our concert actually sounds like in the hall.

Onstage there can be similar problems to the ones in the hall. At times the sound may be transparent on the left, then it booms on the right. One colleague may struggle with his monitor, while another is content. During the sound check, the hall is always empty. But the resonance is totally different once the audience is admitted. This is why right at the start of a concert, the technicians have to react to the musicians' desperate gestures or expressions and try to decipher them as quickly as possible. For this reason it is helpful to travel with your own crew: you know and value each other.

I once experienced a sound fiasco in Dresden's Semperoper, the famous Saxon opera house, during a performance with the German all-star troop Old Friends. I almost ruined the whole concert! What happened? After we found out from our management that we were to play at the Semperoper, we were told that the organizer insisted on a strictly acoustic sound – electric amplification was neither wished for nor was it available. Back to basics. My problem was that there was no such thing in my music. There hadn't been for years. My electric bass relies on amps and speakers, without which it is "bullshit" as my Swiss colleague from Basel would say.

So I played with my equipment – it took a great deal of caution not to push myself into the acoustic foreground.

During the break, the organizer came into our dressing room. "The bass is much too loud!"

I'd been living with this complaint for years. The bass was always considered too loud. Still, I accepted the organizer's impression and toned it down significantly in the second half. Regardless, after the concert ended, the complaints about my bass's volume continued – oddly enough, not from my colleagues onstage. There was a compelling reason for this. Let me explain how the misunderstanding arose.

My colleague, the saxophone player Klaus Doldinger, had told his own sound crew to set up a monitor system onstage exclusively designed for us musicians to hear ourselves better. The sound onstage was what it always was. Poor Albert Mangelsdorff mistakenly believed that the audience could hear him because his trombone sounded loud and clear to him on his monitor. Unbeknownst to us onstage, however, the audience could barely hear the acoustic playing of my colleagues, especially that of Albert Mangelsdorff, who played softly at the best of times, often with a mute: my amplified bass made a pantomime of their performance. We would have been spared this plight if one of the technicians had told us during the sound check that I was too loud. As things stood, though, the technician simply adjusted the sound of the monitors while he was onstage himself. That's how it sometimes goes. Truly galling.

There is no perfect sound without a perfect sound check and no perfect sound check without a good technician. I have no intention of writing a sound check manual here – all I want to do is provide a little insight into the chaotic conditions which, far from being limited to the time before a performance, often prevail throughout the entire evening.

It all revolves around the most perfect sound possible. Distinctions are made as to where the sound belongs. On the one hand, there is the PA or public address system, the sound system for the audience in the hall. But as mentioned before, the term "hall" is far from precise. Are there circles or balconies like in an opera house? And if so, are they only at the back or also to the sides? Unquestionably, concertgoers will insist on the best sound regardless of where they are seated, be it high up, down below, in the back or at the front. While the layperson may believe a few loudspeakers are all it takes to fill up a hall, in practice things are quite different. Often, big loudspeakers "blast" down into the hall, with a few additional ones near the balconies, so that the sides and the gallery are also satisfied. But if the hall is particularly long, an odd trick becomes necessary. We know there is a discrepancy between the optic and the acoustic. The sound of wood being chopped on one side of the street takes a few milliseconds to reach the other. Vision and sound are minimally staggered because light and sound waves travel at different speeds: optic information requires less time to reach the eye than sound does to reach the ear. Assuming the loudspeakers onstage are meant for rows one to forty-five, from row forty-five onwards the sound will get weaker and more tenuous. From there, additional loudspeakers will have to be equipped with sound delay. These speakers delay the sound by a few milliseconds, so that it reaches the listeners in the back in synch with the sound from the speakers onstage, which they have to wait for a few milliseconds longer than the listeners in the first forty-five rows. Ultimately, what happens onstage reaches all listeners in optic and acoustic synchronicity.

Jazz musicians are especially critical when it comes to sound. Advocates of "natural" sound can't bear the slightest alteration – nothing is allowed to change their instrument's original sound. A tall order for sound technicians considering they often have to deal with serious interference. With the United Jazz + Rock Ensemble for instance, six soloists stood right next to each other, each eager to hear their own sound perfectly, regardless of the fact that an instrument much louder than their own was being played in close proximity. This is when so-called "crosstalk" takes place: the sounds being made by one musician get picked up not only by his own microphone, but also by his neighbour's. While some of my colleagues wanted a lot of piano on their monitors, I didn't because I sat closer to the pianist. Others wanted soothing reverberation, but not the trumpeter. As if that wasn't enough, the sound engineer responsible for the hall complained that the loud monitors onstage disturbed the balance in the middle of the hall, where the audience was going to be seated: "Can't you tone it down up there? I can't raise the volume of the bass enough!"

"No can do!"

"I need more of the guitar!"

"Too bad! I only have two possibilities!"

This meant the sound technician responsible for the monitors onstage had only two possible settings: "Who wants to share the monitor sound with the pianist? Who wants to share it with the drummer?"

What a fuss! Things got even worse because, while playing, individual musicians started signalling to the monitor guy that first one thing, then another should be much louder – or softer. Player D became irritated: "Where is the bass drum? All I hear is the drummer's hi-hat – and much too much bass!"

Meanwhile, his neighbour had been happy with the monitor sound: "What's going on? The bass is gone!"

"Sorry, your colleague wanted it softer!"

"Then add it to mine!"

"Can't! I only have two possibilities."

On one occasion, after my loudspeaker system onstage was set to the sound that was perfect for me, it still ended up sounding completely mangled. So much so that I had to refuse to play the concert under these circumstances. What had gone wrong? The drummer, somewhat deaf, had asked for more bass on his monitor because the wind players were covering him up. The fact that these lower frequencies blended together chaotically led to his demand to make the sound much "thinner" on his monitor. So, out with the bass, in with the treble. Under these circumstances, he could hear clearly what I was playing – but the sound of my instrument no longer bore any resemblance to my usual deep bass sound. Since the drummer's stage monitor was set to an extremely high volume, it drowned mine out so badly that I simply had to refuse to put up with his bass sound. While the sound was crystal clear, this version was intolerable: the sound of a bass has nothing to do with glass.

The list of individual demands and requirements is endless – it can drive sound engineers to despair.

Even if we assume that, eventually, general satisfaction is achieved during the sound check, there still is no end in sight: the settings adjusted in an empty hall need to be adapted once the audience is present. If the hall is full, as one would hope, nothing "carries" anymore, everything has gone "dry." More reverberation! But soloist A wants much more reverberation than soloist B. Soloist C wants a slight delay, but there can't be any crosstalk with soloist B's microphone. Misunderstandings and frustration abound.

With the Garbarek Group, our team of sound engineers was so experienced that in some concert halls our two technicians didn't even require our presence for the sound check. One was a bass player himself, the other a drummer – both were experts. After a few years, we were so attuned to each other, that we had blind faith in their sound.

Still, there is no such thing as guaranteed perfection. Too many imponderables! For a period of about one whole year, there was something wrong with my equipment. It drove me mad almost every single night, requiring constant attention without ever giving any clue as to what might be causing the problem. Every time I started to play a longer solo, loud cracking and whistling would become audible. The only way to put an end to it was to quickly switch my amp off and back on again – with lightning speed.

Expert discussions led to no insights – only to theories. The problem was that none of them could be confirmed. I contacted the makers of all my equipment, hoping they would be able to establish a remote diagnosis. Far from it!

I was on the verge of throwing everything away and replacing it, which would have cost me dearly.

Finally, a technician figured out that a chip in my delay was reacting to voltage variation in the network, caused, among other things, by the light dimmers. That explained why my equipment failed me at the start of every solo: every time the stage light shining on the whole band was dimmed to focus only on me, the chip reacted by cracking. I can assure you it was sheer agony waiting for this malfunction to occur night after night for almost a year without knowing what was causing it. Understandably, my focus on the less technical, more musical aspects of performing was lost. The mystery had just been solved – I was on the road again with perfectly functioning equipment – when in 2007 fate chimed in: "Enough is enough! Things can't go on forever!"

Now my perfect arsenal rests in a corner of my home studio, where it is dusted at regular intervals. There isn't anything else I can do with it.

At some point, every musician starts tinkering around with their instrument and equipment in their quest for perfection. Does perfection even exist? It has to! It's only that no one ever finds it! The "perfect" instrument calls for the perfect pickup. Usually, it's built in. How does the perfect sound reach the amplifier? Through the perfect cable. This has to be shielded and coated, with gold-plated plugs at either end, so that corrosion won't hinder his perfect sound. On to the next problem: the amplifier. Should it be the most expensive one or should it be good value? Light or heavy? Does size matter after all? How many auxiliary controls does it have? Testing is only possible if the perfect loudspeaker is connected via the perfect cable. Finally, a decision can be made. Who decides? Where? Does he do it in the living room or in the store? In a club or in a concert hall? With or without audience? In the front, in the back, high up, down below? Is the picture of the chimera we jazz musicians are forever chasing clear enough yet? Our eternal search for ever more sophisticated technology to mask our own shortcomings?

What a blessing it is that we have the capacity to adapt. Twice only in my musical life have I left a hall as a listener because the sound was hopelessly inadequate. And it must be added that I was the only one of the malcontents, or the first, at any rate, to leave the venue. On all other occasions, I was able to rely on my auditory organs' capacity to adapt. Once, there was a concert with John McLaughlin's first ensemble, the legendary Mahavishnu Ensemble, in a Frankfurt exhibition hall that certainly wasn't built for acoustic purposes. Initially, it sounded dreadful. But my doubts were cast aside by my curiosity about the musicians, none of whom I was familiar with. I was surprised by how much had been invested in visual effects. Spotlights followed each active musician: a drum roll would start in total darkness; then, the light shining on the drum would slowly grow to encompass the entire band as it dramatically started to play. A brilliantly effective choreography! It seemed to help the audience forget about the lousy sound – or to deflect from it at the very least. Funnily enough, from the second half of the performance, I found the sound to be perfectly tolerable. Had the crew managed to significantly improve the sound or had my brain adapted to the substandard acoustics? It didn't matter – by the end of the evening, I felt like I had attended a great concert. If even we, the musicians, can't agree on anything, reaching different conclusions time and time again, how is the audience supposed to form an opinion?

This will have to do. As promised, I have no intention of writing a sound check manual! Complaints backstage during the breaks and after concerts are legendary – they have no place here. Readers will have to content themselves with this tiny snippet of the imponderables of sound – enjoying performances is easier with an open mind.

Now then, time for my worst onstage sound. It was produced for a concert in Warsaw. I was playing in a trio with Michael Naura on piano and Wolfgang Schlüter on vibraphone. I loved Naura's warm sound on the Fender Rhodes electric piano – he had a feel for sound and harmonies, but hearing him on the grand piano was new to me. To my taste, he was better on the Fender Rhodes. Pianists, however, disagree on this count as they consider the grand piano the queen of all instruments. Too bad that some things can't really be done on a grand piano: a chord won't last for more than ten seconds no matter how brutally you pound the keys. It's even worse if there are other instruments playing along: they will drown out the fading chord. All pianists react the same way at this point: they start noodling around to prolong the sound, but nothing lasting is ever produced. As dexterity is part of the skillset required to play the piano, they continue in this vein, which logically leads to a rather jittery sequence. I was never able to shake the feeling that pianists, too, want continuous sounds; these, however, can only be produced electrically.

Time to get back to the *Warsaw Concerto* – no, the concert in Warsaw.

I wasn't familiar with the technology in the hall; I only knew my own and the sound that went with it. This was precisely what I presented during the sound check. But when the local technicians connected my equipment to theirs, my acoustic amplification was blamed for the deplorable sound in the hall. For the last time ever, I made the mistake of following the instructions of technicians I didn't know. I adjusted my sound onstage until the technicians in the hall were clearly satisfied. So far, so good. The only problem: my sound onstage was now pitiful. With sound like this I couldn't even come close to meeting my usual standards. Even if you're not dealing with a Stradivarius, there are a few basic requirements when it comes to quality. You can't play a Bach suite on a cigar box with strings. Even if you're Pablo Casals.

I can't remember why I didn't object. To make things worse, during my rather unsuccessful performance, I saw Jan Garbarek's band in the wings – with all my future Scandinavian colleagues. There they stood, witnessing my misery. That's what it must feel like when you're being taken to the scaffold. Luckily, Jan heard me again later, on other occasions – or he never would have asked me to join his new band.

My best concert? What can I remember? There isn't a clear favourite, but one solo performance at the KITO, a jazz club in Bremen's Vegesack district, stands out. While I was setting up my equipment on the wooden stage, I realized that my stage monitors wouldn't be enough for the premises. I had to get connected to the venue's public address system, the PA, which, annoyingly, used to be called "vocal system"[1] in German. I don't know what my concert eventually sounded like in the audience, but the large, powerful subwoofer I placed under the stage produced very warm lows onstage. I can honestly say that I have never had a better, more potent, more powerful, warmer or fuller sound onstage! Had it been up to me, I never would have stopped playing! Although I can't prove it, I suspect that it must have been an exceptionally good solo concert. If this really was the case, the audience wouldn't have known why. As an old stager, I knew that it was the exact location at which I

---

1. *Gesangsanlage.*

found myself onstage that afforded me this pleasure. Listeners can't extrapolate what we, the musicians, play or why we play it one way or another. There were many concerts during which I felt that I had had particularly good ideas, only to later hear backstage: "It really didn't go well today."

Just as often, the opposite would happen. I'd struggle to come up with ideas, relying on routine alone, but after the show, people would say: "Today was even better than usual!"

We all experienced this regularly. Perhaps it's better this way – that your perception of quality should be so subjective, so dependent on your mood. Jazz musicians are only human, after all. Just like athletes, who spend years practising for a particular event, only to be unwell when it finally takes place. What's wrong with the second horn in the top symphony orchestra today? The celebrated guitarist isn't playing as well as usual; what's wrong with him tonight?

Questions like these can be asked in any genre. Only top performances are deemed acceptable. Would it be tolerated if a performance, a concert was cancelled simply because someone was feeling off that day? I'm afraid not. If you've signed up for an event, you participate in it, even if the chance to "blow away" the audience is remote. It's only after I started playing professionally that I inevitably had to deal with situations like these. Before that, I took it for granted that people like Oscar Peterson and his bass player Ray Brown would always be in peak form. Anything else would have been unacceptable – regardless of colds or trouble at home or on the road. Later on, I learned the hard way that it was good to have acquired a familiar routine, just in case, so that you could keep any potential calamities to yourself – in short, so you could be a pro and hide any weaknesses.

I have never cancelled a concert. But during the time I gave bass solo concerts, it happened frequently towards the end that a mysterious, bothersome "player's block" would prevent me from playing a melody so simple I could have played it in my sleep before. As a jazz musician, I have the good fortune of being able to make changes at any time. As a rule, I could generally hide that something was wrong. These lapses did, however, lead me to give up my successful solo performances. Unfortunately, I never had the chance to ask a classical performer if lapses of this sort can occur in their line of work, too, and what reactions they elicit.

In the early 1970s, while I was working on my first ECM release, *The Colours of Chloë*, I also experienced a kind of emptiness. All the different parts were ready. Only a short segue from one part to another was still missing. A bass solo was meant to do the trick – this was what I'd decided. But everything I came up with sounded banal, take after take, try after try – nothing but bland phrases. I was getting desperate. At least I can say today that after countless attempts, I eventually succeeded. I will take care not to divulge the location of this segue.

In situations like these, it was a huge relief to be able to talk to colleagues who had experienced something similar. Jan Garbarek also reported strange things about himself. On one occasion, he couldn't make a single sound with his instrument even though he was blowing enough air into it. Luckily for us, these issues didn't become permanent. Among my acquaintances, I also heard of an extremely successful graphic artist who would spend hours in front of a blank sheet of paper without so much as a single idea. At moments like these, you believe that all your talent is lost. Be it writers' block, painters' block, musicians' block or speakers' block, how can it be that one day everything works just fine, and the next, not at all?

On the other hand, there was also a particular repetitive effect which I never managed to create with my right hand. It wasn't just a question of speed – this, in fact, wasn't an issue. One day, however, during the concert in Bremen mentioned earlier, I unexpectedly managed this technique – with the greatest of ease. Everything went smoothly. It was basically a miracle – the spell was broken. I could repeat the effect at a whim. Finally! I tried again and again, all evening long – it worked every single time. Perfect!

The following night – we were on tour – it was as if nothing had ever happened. My fingers were floundering again. Nothing had been learned. To hell with the mind!

In my youth, when I often listened to concerts on the radio with my father, silence once filled the airwaves during a piano concert. We only found out why a few days later: the famous pianist had had a blackout and couldn't remember what came next. The conductor took his musical score, left the stand and showed the poor woman the place where she'd got stuck. Shortly thereafter, the concert resumed. I hope I never have to find out how one gets over a blackout of this sort…

As an improviser, I have never had anything to do with such unfortunate incidents. But in jazz, too, it's embarrassing if I forget that a melody shouldn't be played just once, that it ought to be repeated. Naturally, this can only happen when playing in an ensemble. But when it does, the key is to react as quickly as possible and identify the error. Since everyone is familiar with lapses of this kind, tolerance can be expected from one's colleagues. It only takes a short time to join them at the right place in the piece. After their brief wait is over, their chastising expressions alone reveal the frustration and annoyance they feel when a routine performance is disrupted and, for a second, it isn't clear how total chaos can be averted. On a different note, I can't remember the audience ever signalling to us how hairy a situation might have been. Bear in mind that it is only a matter of a few seconds. A jarring note barely has the time to reach the ear of an audience member before it is already over. We alone, the perpetrators onstage, can gauge the magnitude of what has just been prevented.

With hindsight, it's only now that I realize how routine many parts of my working life had become over the last few years. I keep remembering my first studio experiences with the Erwin Lehn Big Band, and how irritated I was by the worldly-wise attitude of many of my colleagues when I was a young musician. Eventually, it was this routine that helped me lead the life of a professional musician. But on many occasions, it also made one concert seem just like another. Life on the road leads to monotony. The specifics get lost when you travel every day, checking into different hotels, following the same procedures – over a hundred times a year.

For something to be memorable, it has to be striking or unusual. When the danger of falling into a rut grew too real, I had to remind myself that many concertgoers spent weeks or even months looking forward to a particular concert – of course they expected the musicians to put their heart and soul into the performance they would attend. They would have been shocked to find out what the mood backstage was like sometimes: "If only it was over!"

"Can we cut it short tonight?"

These things do happen, I admit. But thoughts like these would always vanish into thin air as soon as a concert started – I was spellbound, every time.

Postlude

It's been eight years since I was last able to play the bass. This may be hard to imagine for the healthy "average citizen." Initially, I still thought about going on, differently, by playing more calmly, more slowly, at a leisurely pace – within the bounds of my limited possibilities.

It became clear to me very soon that this would remain a dream. On the one hand, because the nerve cells in the brain responsible for controlling muscles can't be repaired. On the other hand, because flexibility is irretrievably lost when you reach a certain age – even if, by means of absurd exertions, some degree of agility might be restored. Every year, a quarter of a million people suffer a stroke in Germany alone – a frightful number. In spite of this, stroke symptoms had never been on my mind before. I really had no idea. I didn't even know the difference between a stroke and a heart attack. I didn't know what goes on in the two halves of the brain, that each is responsible for the other side of the body. I didn't know that a dysfunction on the left side can cause speech loss and affect memory. I didn't know any of this.

At least, I retained my memory and the ability to speak. Initially, "only" my movements were restricted. Other consequences didn't become noticeable until later. I still had an appetite, but I didn't really get hungry anymore. My feelings were affected, too: if something funny happened, I couldn't stop laughing, especially if it involved awkward *schadenfreude*. A female patient I met in rehab experienced the same thing. When we saw each other in the clinic's corridors in our wheelchairs, we would laugh so hard, we cried – for no reason at all. Nothing too bad, in principle: the opposite can happen, as well. This was the case with another patient, who, even though I was smiling, burst into tears when I wished her a good morning on the way to the breakfast room. Heightened emotional states can be common. Before the stroke, this would have been inconceivable. Let's put it this way: in my case, the process unfolded graciously.

There are hopeless cases, too. In my rehab clinic, there was a whole floor reserved for these unfortunate patients. What misery I could observe from my wheelchair when the ambulance brought in new patients almost every day! In contrast, I could consider myself in great health. After all, I was merely unfit for work.

In the first three months, therapy has to be the most intensive: daily and continuous, so that new nerves can form and hopefully reactivate the muscles. Unfortunately, this training becomes more and more difficult with older patients, and their chances of recovery slimmer. This does not mean, however, that it is better to suffer a stroke when you are younger.

After the initial three months of "intensive care," another three months can lead to more modest successes, but after that, there is a steady downward trend. Progress is still possible, but it requires more and more effort, often accompanied by frustration. This is how it was and – worse yet – still is with me.

A stroke can manifest as seemingly absurd disorders at times. When I walk, for instance, my affected arm rises towards my chin while my fingers form a fist. It is only when I stand still that the arm can relax again, hanging by my side. During one of my later attempts to walk down the long corridors of the clinic (at some point the therapist urges you to get out of your wheelchair), I met another patient, whose arm hung by his side, straight. I approached him: "My dear colleague, I envy you your straight arm. How do you do it? Mine curls up all the time."

My interlocutor reacted surprised: "You must be joking! I envy you. The reason I can't raise my arm is that it's paralysed…"

The days are long in a rehab clinic. There is much time to think. And it is quiet. That, mind you, never bothered me: I have never had a radio in any of my apartments, and I still don't.

Nothing tootles on incessantly in the background. Perhaps this is at the core of the successful career I've had – my whole life, I've had to listen in order to know whether something is worth it or not. No constant stream trickling through the airwaves. No radio alarm clock to wake me up. No tootling radio in the bathroom. My breakfast? I enjoy it in silence. What effort the ladies and gentlemen of pop put into producing the perfect sound – only for the radio to go on squawking ceaselessly, without anyone even paying attention.

As far as I'm concerned, music isn't relaxation. It is its polar opposite: tension and concentration. There is no room for relaxation. ECM's slogan, "The most beautiful sound next to silence," applies perfectly to me. Silence is wonderful – as a musician, you have to try hard to top it.

The only thing that interrupted the quiet at the rehab clinic was the daily therapy, during which I received astonishingly naïve suggestions from the experts. Since movement in my left hand was so severely restricted, wasn't it worth considering changing sides? The right hand could hold the fingerboard, while the fingers of the left plucked at the strings. One therapist suggested I give up plucking altogether, using the bow, instead – most certainly not a jazz expert.

Figure 36: Jan Garbarek and Eberhard Weber during their first encounter after Weber's stroke. Open-air Jazz in Junas (southern France), 2014

On my request, my special bass was brought to me in the rehab clinic. I wanted to find out if there was any chance that I might be able to use the instrument again in a meaningful way.

I was still in a wheelchair back then. Getting out of it was difficult, as was sitting on a stool the way I used to when I played. The bass was set up in my room, ready to let me know if this would work or not. By now I had become quite good at using the wheelchair. It was actually fun manoeuvring it through the corridors, making turns, turning around. But one day, as I was reversing into my room, the fun got out of hand. I heard something fall and shatter – I'd forgotten about the bass and knocked it over. The sounds of breakage didn't bode well. The strings dangled limply – the neck was broken. So much for my dream of playing again.

Fortunately, there are various connections between professional musicians that make it possible to find quick fixes. I was put in touch with the luthier of the Berlin Philharmonic – it didn't get any better than that. A long cab ride brought me to him. After beholding the unusual instrument, the luthier buckled down to the task. A couple of days later, the bass was successfully repaired. The cost of my mishap was considerable: two never-ending taxi rides and one perfect repair. I learned my lesson: backing up in a wheelchair takes some skill.

When you are young, old age seems far away, incredibly far away. In the time I was active, I never gave any thought to securing a retirement income by means of a professorship, for instance. Now I know: a few euros more each month certainly brighten the mood once you reach a certain age. This is something I never thought of in the past: I was healthy. I wanted to play, not teach. It could go on like this forever.

But there is another reason, an entirely profane reason, why I have never wanted to take on a professorship. I have always been of the following opinion (in a mysterious way it has taken on a new meaning today): I can't play the bass. But I know how it's done!

Discography

Eberhard Weber – **Once Upon a Time**

    Eberhard Weber: bass
    Recorded live in Avignon, August 1994
    ECM 2699

Hommage à Eberhard Weber
    Pat Metheny: guitars
    Jan Garbarek: soprano saxophone
    Gary Burton: vibraphone
    Scott Colley: double bass
    Danny Gottlieb: drums
    Paul McCandless: English horn, soprano saxophone
    Klaus Graf: alto saxophone
    Ernst Hutter: euphonium
    SWR Big Band
    Michael Gibbs: arranger, conductor
    Helge Sunde: conductor
    Recorded January 2015
    ECM 2463

Eberhard Weber – **Encore**
Eberhard Weber: bass, keyboards
Ack van Rooyen: flugelhorn
Recorded 1990–2014
ECM 2439

Eberhard Weber – **Résumé**
Eberhard Weber: bass, keyboards
Jan Garbarek: soprano and tenor saxophones, Selje flute
Michael DiPasqua: drums, percussion
Recorded 1990–2007
ECM 2051

Eberhard Weber – **Stages Of A Long Journey**
Jan Garbarek: soprano and tenor saxophones
Gary Burton: vibraphone

Rainer Brüninghaus: piano
Wolfgang Dauner: piano
Eberhard Weber: bass, double bass
Marilyn Mazur: percussion
Reto Weber: hang
Nino G.: beatbox
SWR Stuttgart Radio Symphony Orchestra
Roland Kluttig: conductor
Recorded March 2005
ECM 1920

Eberhard Weber – **Endless Days**
Eberhard Weber: bass
Paul McCandless: oboe, English horn, bass clarinet, soprano saxophone
Rainer Brüninghaus: piano, keyboards
Michael DiPasqua: drums, percussion
Recorded April 2000
ECM 1748

Eberhard Weber – **Pendulum**
Eberhard Weber: bass
Recorded Spring 1993
ECM 1518

Eberhard Weber – **Orchestra**
Eberhard Weber: bass, percussion, keyboards
Herbert Joos, Anton Jillich: flugelhorns
Rudolf Diebetsberger, Thomas Hauschild: French horns
Wolfgang Czelustra, Andreas Richter: trombones
Winfried Rapp: bass trombone
Franz Stagl: tuba
Recorded May and August 1988
ECM 1374

Eberhard Weber – **Chorus**
Eberhard Weber: bass, synthesizer
Jan Garbarek: soprano and tenor saxophones
Ralf Hübner: drums
Recorded September 1984
ECM 1288

Eberhard Weber – **Later That Evening**
Eberhard Weber: bass
Paul McCandless: soprano saxophone, oboe, English horn, bass clarinet
Bill Frisell: guitar
Lyle Mays: piano
Michael DiPasqua: drums, percussion
Recorded March 1982
ECM 1231

Eberhard Weber Colours – **Little Movements**
Charlie Mariano: soprano saxophone, flute
Rainer Brüninghaus: piano, synthesizer
Eberhard Weber: bass
John Marshall: drums, percussion

Recorded July 1980
ECM 1186

Eberhard Weber – **Fluid Rustle**
Eberhard Weber: bass, tarang
Bonnie Herman: voice
Norma Winstone: voice
Gary Burton: vibraharp, marimba
Bill Frisell: guitar, balalaika
Recorded January 1979
ECM 1137

Eberhard Weber – **Silent Feet**
Charlie Mariano: soprano saxophone, flute
Rainer Brüninghaus: piano, synthesizer
Eberhard Weber: bass
John Marshall: drums, percussion
Recorded November 1977
ECM 1107

Eberhard Weber – **The Following Morning**
Eberhard Weber: bass
Rainer Brüninghaus: piano
Members of the Philharmonic Orchestra Oslo
Recorded August 1976
ECM 1084

Eberhard Weber – **Yellow Fields**
Charlie Mariano: soprano saxophone, shenai, nagaswaram
Rainer Brüninghaus: keyboards
Eberhard Weber: bass
Jon Christensen: drums
Recorded September 1975
ECM 1066

Eberhard Weber – **The Colours Of Chloë**
Eberhard Weber: bass, cello, ocarina
Rainer Brüninghaus: piano, synthesizer
Peter Giger: drums, percussion
Ralf Hübner: drums
Ack van Rooyen: flugelhorn
Cellos of the Südfunk Symphony Orchestra Stuttgart
Recorded December 1973
ECM 1042

Eberhard Weber – **Colours**
Yellow Fields | Silent Feet | Little Movements
Recorded September 1975, November 1977 and July 1980
ECM 2133–35

Eberhard Weber – **Selected Recordings**
Recorded 1974–2000
ECM:rarum XVIII

Eberhard Weber – **Works**
An Anthology
Released 1985

As a guest (selection):

The Gary Burton Quartet w/Eberhard Weber – **Passengers**
Gary Burton: vibraharp
Pat Metheny: guitar
Steve Swallow: bass guitar
Dan Gottlieb: drums
Eberhard Weber: bass
Recorded November 1976
ECM 1092

The Gary Burton Quintet w/Eberhard Weber – **Ring**
Gary Burton: vibraharp
Mick Goodrick: guitar
Pat Metheny: guitars
Steve Swallow: bass guitar
Bob Moses: percussion
Eberhard Weber: bass
Recorded July 1974
ECM 1051

Wolfgang Dauner – **Output**
Wolfgang Dauner: piano, clavinet
Fred Braceful: percussion, voice
Eberhard Weber: bass, cello, guitar
Recorded September 1970
ECM 1006

Jan Garbarek – **Rites**
Jan Garbarek: soprano and tenor saxophones, synthesizers, samplers, percussion
Rainer Brüninghaus: piano, keyboard
Eberhard Weber: bass
Marilyn Mazur: drums, percussion
Jansug Kakhidze: singer, conductor
Tbilisi Symphony Orchestra
Bugge Wesseltoft: synthesizer, electronic effects, accordion
Boys from the choir Sølvguttene
Recorded March 1998
ECM 1685/86

Jan Garbarek – **Visible World**
Jan Garbarek: soprano and tenor saxophones, electronic keyboard, percussion, Meraaker clarinet
Rainer Brüninghaus: piano, synthesizer
Eberhard Weber: bass
Marilyn Mazur: percussion, drums
Manu Katché: drums
Trilok Gurtu: tabla
Mari Boine: vocal
Recorded June 1995
ECM 1585

Jan Garbarek Group – **Twelve Moons**
Jan Garbarek: soprano and tenor saxophones, keyboards
Rainer Brüninghaus: keyboards

Eberhard Weber: bass
Manu Katché: drums
Marilyn Mazur: percussion
Agnes Buen Garnås: vocal
Mari Boine: vocal
Recorded September 1992
ECM 1500

Jan Garbarek – **I Took Up The Runes**
Jan Garbarek: soprano and tenor saxophones
Rainer Brüninghaus: piano
Eberhard Weber: bass
Nana Vasconcelos: percussion
Manu Katché: drums
Bugge Wesseltoft: synthesizer
Ingor Ántte Áilu Gaup: voice
Recorded August 1990
ECM 1419

Jan Garbarek – **Legend Of The Seven Dreams**
Jan Garbarek: soprano and tenor saxophones, flute, percussion
Rainer Brüninghaus: keyboards
Nana Vasconcelos: percussion, voice
Eberhard Weber: bass
Recorded July 1988
ECM 1381

Jan Garbarek Group – **It's OK To Listen To The Gray Voice**
Jan Garbarek: tenor and soprano saxophones
David Torn: guitars, guitar synthesizer, DX 7
Eberhard Weber: bass
Michael DiPasqua: drums, percussion
Recorded December 1984
ECM 1294

Jan Garbarek Group – **Wayfarer**
Jan Garbarek: tenor and soprano saxophones
Bill Frisell: guitar
Eberhard Weber: bass
Michael DiPasqua: drums, percussion
Recorded March 1983
ECM 1259

Jan Garbarek Group – **Paths, Prints**
Jan Garbarek: tenor and soprano saxophones, wood flutes, percussion
Bill Frisell: guitar
Eberhard Weber: bass
Jon Christensen: drums, percussion
Recorded December 1981
ECM 1223

Jan Garbarek Group – **Photo With ...**
Jan Garbarek: tenor and soprano saxophones
Bill Connors: guitar
John Taylor: piano

Eberhard Weber: bass
Jon Christensen: drums
Recorded December 1978
ECM 1135

Jazzensemble des Hessischen Rundfunks – **Atmospheric Conditions Permitting**
Tony Scott, Karel Krautgartner, Theo Jörgensmann, Rüdiger Carl: clarinets
Michel Pilz: bass clarinet
Christof Lauer, Emil Mangelsdorff, Lee Konitz, Joki Freund, Günter Kronberg: saxophones
Heinz Sauer: soprano, alto and tenor saxophones, drum computer, synthesizer
Thomas Heberer, Ulrich Beckerhoff: trumpets
Günter Christmann, Albert Mangelsdorff: trombones
Peter Kowald: tuba
Bill Frisell, Volker Kriegel: guitars
Alexander von Schlippenbach, Bob Degen, Hans Lüdemann, Milcho Leviev: pianos
Rainer Brüninghaus: electric piano, synthesizer
Theodossij Spassov: kaval
Eberhard Weber: bass
Alois Kott, Günter Lenz, Thomas Heidepriem,
Buschi Niebergall, Adelhard Roidinger: double basses
Ralf Hübner, Paul Lovens, Peter Giger, Detlef Schönenberg: drums
Wilhelm Liefland: narrator
Recorded 1967–1993
ECM 1549/50

Pat Metheny – **Watercolors**
Pat Metheny: guitars
Lyle Mays: piano
Eberhard Weber: bass
Dan Gottlieb: drums
Recorded February 1977
ECM 1097

Michael Naura – **Vanessa**
Michael Naura: piano
Wolfgang Schlüter: vibraphone, marimba, percussion
Eberhard Weber: bass
Joe Nay: drums
Klaus Thunemann: bassoon
Recorded September 1974
ECM 1053

Peter Rühmkorf – **Kein Apolloprogramm für Lyrik**
Michael Naura: piano
Wolfgang Schlüter: vibraphone, marimba
Eberhard Weber: bass, cello

Ralph Towner Solstice – **Sound And Shadows**
Ralph Towner: 12-string and classical guitars, piano, French horn
Jan Garbarek: soprano and tenor saxophones, flute
Eberhard Weber: bass, cello
Jon Christensen: drums
Recorded February 1977
ECM 1095

Ralph Towner – **Solstice**
Ralph Towner: 12-string and classical guitars, piano
Jan Garbarek: tenor and soprano saxophones, flute
Eberhard Weber: bass, cello
Jon Christensen: drums, percussion
Recorded December 1974
ECM 1060

Mal Waldron – **The Call**
Mal Waldron: electric piano
Jimmy Jackson: organ
Eberhard Weber: bass
Fred Braceful: drums
Recorded February 1971
JAPO 60001

Index

Abercrombie, John 89, 98, 115–16
Alexander, Monty 72, 74
Amazon (river) 12
Anderson, Arild 111
An Evening with Vincent Van Ritz 97
Asmussen, Svend 58
Australia 120–21, **123**, 124

Bach, J. S. 21, 23–24
Baden-Baden 68–69
Baden-Powell 72
Baker, Chet 75
banjo 17–18
Bargeron, Dave 86
Bates, Norman 33
Baumeister, Peter 83
Beethoven
    Fifth Symphony 11, 18
Berendt, Joachim-Ernst 16, 68–70
Berger, Karl 66
Berlin 1, 19, 100, 170
    Charité Hospital 1, 3–5, 7
    Jazz Festival 100
    Median Clinic, Grünheide 7
    Philharmonic Hall 1, 3–4, 100–101
    Swissotel 2
    Wilmersdorf 17
Beyreuth Festival 27
Bielefeld
    Ulmenwall Bunker 146
Blood, Sweat & Tears 86

blues (12 bar) 13–14
Bombay 151–52
Boston 108, 117
    Berklee College of Music 102, 125
Boyle, Gary 100
Braceful, Fred **51**, 52, 63–64, **65**
Brandes, Vera 113–14
Brazil 84
    Brazilian music 10, 93
Bremen
    KITO club 163, 165
Brötzmann, Peter 69
Brown, Ray 52–53, 78, 164
Brubeck, Dave 33
Brüninghaus, Rainer 2, 5, 22, 85–86, 96,
    100, 112, **121**, **123**, 124
    with Garbarek 125–26, 143
Brunner-Schwer, Hans Georg 72, 74
Burton, Gary 2, 102, 111, 117
    Passengers 102
    Quintet tours 104, 108–10, 115, 118,
        122
    Ring 102
Bush, Kate 75, 137–38, **139**

Carr, Ian 114, 131, **134**
Cavalli, Pierre 59
Chambers, Paul 52
Chorus 73, 97
Christensen, Jon 112, 114, 125
Clare, Kenny 72

Clarke, Stanley 111, 118
Colours (band) 34, 86, 110, 112–15, **116**, **123**, 128, 149
   break up of 124
   in Australia/NZ 124
   in USA 115–17
Colours of Chloë 92, 94, 96–97, 100, 102, 109–10, 112, 164
Copenhagen
   Jazzhus Montmartre **136**
Corea, Chick 100

Daniel, Yuri 8, 128
Danielsson, Palle 98, 111, 115, 125
Dankworth, John 22
Dauner, Wolfgang 2, 46, 49–50, 52, 57, 59, **61**, 63, 75, 79, 85, 93, 107, 131, **132**, 133, **134**, **136**
   Dream Talk 53
   free jazz experiments 64, 68–69
   and LSD 135
   Trio **51**, 59, 62, 80, 94
Dautel, Fritz, **50**
Davis, Miles 35
DeJohnette, Jack 108, 112
Desmond, Paul 33
DIFA (film company) 46, **47**
DiPasqua, Michael 12–**13**, **107**, 125, 143, **144**, 157
Dixieland jazz 9–10
Doldinger, Klaus 159
double bass, 10, 14
   cello tuning 16
   electric double bass 14
Double Image (quartet) 13
Dresden
   Semperoper 158–59
Durham (UK) 130–31
Düsseldorf
   Philipshalle 133

ECM (record company) 2, 9, 73–74, 89–90, 94, 97–98, 105, 108–109, 112, 114, 119, 164
   musicians on label 108, 115
   office of 95, 99
Edelhagen, Kurt 83

Edinburgh 147
Egan, Mark 111
Eicher, Manfred 87, 94, **95**, 96–99
Ellington, Duke 34
Encore 97
Esslingen am Neckar (home town) 19, 22–23, 28, 80, 83–84, 157
   Alte Reichsstadt 41
   Georgii Gymnasium 25, 29–32, 36, 41, 44, 54, 67
   in American occupation zone 25–26
Etté, Bernard 17–18
Evans, Bill 53

Favre, Pierre 69
Fischer, Horst, 42–43
Frankfurt 84
   Centennial Hall 70, 135
   US Consulate 104–5
free jazz 62–69
Freund, Joki 79
Friesen, David 111
Frisell, Bill 89, **107**, 125, 147, 157
Froboess, Conny 50–51
Fruth, Willi 72, 77

Garbarek, Jan 2, 5, 58, 73–74, 94–94, 105, 125–26, 128, 143, **144**, 148, 150, **155**, 157, 163, 165, **169**
   duo with 127
   Group 1, 5, 7–8, 58, 125–29, 136–37, 142, 149, 161
   Scandinavian quartet 98, 163
Gerhardt, Paul 24
Gibbs, Mike 125
Giger, Peter 96
Goethe Institute 84, 127–28, 150, 154
Gomez, Eddie 110
Goodman, Benny 34
Gottlieb, Danny 108
Great German Record Prize 97
Gröbenzell 97, **98**
Gruntz, George 57
Gulda, Friedrich 35–36
Gurtu, Trilok 5
Gutesha, Mladen 100

Haden, Charlie 111, 115
Hamburg 78, 80
	Fabrik 106
	State Opera 27
Hamma, Walter (luthier) 54–55
Hancock, Herbie 101
Hawes, Hampton, 72
Hellman, Marc 84
Hessischer Rundfunk 79
HGBS *see* Brunner-Schwer, Hans Georg
Hiseman, Jon 131, 133, **134**
Hitler, Adolf 18–19
Hoffman, Herr (music teacher) 31, 36
Hohensee, Peter 2–5
Holland, Dave 111
Hübner, Ralf 73–74, 96, 100, 147, 150

IBM advertising department 83
Intercontinental 72
Inzalaco, Tony 83
Izenzon, David 108

Jankowski, Horst 42–43, 46, 49
	Singers 46, 49
Jansson, Lars 125
Jarrett, Keith 11, 99, 115, 117, 125
jazz (definitions of) 9–10, 14, 16, 62
Jazzthetik (magazine) 2
Johns, Bibi 51
Johnson, Marc 111

Karg, Jürgen 63
Kissler, Arno 40, **41**
Knieper, Reinhard 101
Knispel, Siggi 51
Kongshaug, Jan Erik 95
Kriegel, Ev 78, 83, 85, **87**, 119
Kriegel, Volker 78–80, 83–87, 90, 113,
	115, 131, 133, **134**, **136**
	Missing Link 114
Kronburg, Günter 79
Kuhn, Steve 89

LaFaro, Scott, 53–54
Lahore 150–51
Later That Evening (album) 137
Lehn, Erwin 42–44, 53, 166

Leinstoll, Achim **50**
Lippman, Horst 52
Lippmann, Theo **50**
Lübeck 7
Ludwigsburg-Eglosheim
	Sound Studio Bauer 95–96
'Lullaby of Birdland' 37–39
luthiers 15, 54, 170

McCandless, Paul 102, **103**, **107**, 115
McLaughlin, John 162
Madrid 84
Mahavishnu Orchestra 162
Mangelsdorff, Albert 59, 62, 69–70, 75, 79,
	131, **134**, 159
Mangelsdorff, Emil 59
Mariano, Charlie 34, 93, 112–**13**, **120**,
	122, **123**, 124, 131, 148
Marseilles 7
Marshall, John 75, 114–15, **121**, **123**
Mauer, Norbert 7
Mays, Lyle **107**
Mazur, Marilyn 2
Menza, Don 59
Metheny, Pat 104, 122
Metzger, Hans-Arnold 21
Mild Maniac 86
Miller, Brian 100
Mingus, Charles 34
Mitchell, Red 15–16, 58
Moore, Glen 111
Morello, Joe 33
Mosch, Ernst 42–43
Motian, Paul 53, 96, 115, 125
MPS (record company) 72, 74, 76–77, 86,
	94
Mumbai *see* Bombay
Munich 10, 111, 126
	Circus Krone 111
	Domicile 146
	Herkules Hall 127–28
	Philharmonic Hall 101
	US Consulate 105

Naura, Michael 85, 106–7, 162
Nay, Joe 85–86
NDR (radio station) 78, 80, 84, 137

Neumeier, Mani 66
New Orleans jazz 9
New York
    Avery Fisher Hall 116
Nino G 2
Nucleus 114–15

Oregon (band) 115, 137
Oslo
    Rainbow Studio 95

Pass, Joe 72
Pastorius, Jaco 111, 118
Patitucci, John 111
Pauly, Walter 115
Peacock, Gary 111
Pendulum 139
Peterson, Oscar 52–53, 164
Pettiford, Oscar 15
Philadelphia 108
Pike, Dave 9
    (New) Dave Pike Set 83–85, 107
Pont du Gard 13
Ponty, Jean-Luc 59, **61**

Ranglin, Ernest 74
Real Book 109
recording technology 71, 75–76
Redman, Dewey 115
Résumé (album) 82, 97
Rettenbacher, Hans 83
Romano, Aldo **61**
Rome 141
Rypdal, Terje 115

SABA (record company) 72
Sauer, Heinz 79
Schaffner, Roland 84
Schäuble, Carl Johann (brother-in-law)
    23, 46
Schlüter, Wolfgang 162–63
Schochow, Klaus (cousin) 27, 58–59
Schoof, Manfred 51, 59, 62, 69
Schretzmeier, Werner 131, **132**
Schwäble, Martin 21–22, 36, **37**, 39, 41,
    47
SDR 93, 100, 131
Shearing, George 37

Shorter, Wayne 111
Soft Machine 115
Solti, Sir Georg 140–41
Spectrum 86–87, 92, 107, 112, 115, 124
Stages of a Long Journey 2
Stenson, Bobo 98
Stern, Leni (Magdalena Thora) 131
Stöwsand, Thomas 94, 99
Stuttgart 19, 46, 59, 73–74
    Liederhalle 22, 75, 101
    SDR Stuttgart Dance Orchestra 42–44
    Stuttgart-Hedelfingen 19
    Stuttgart Philharmonic 18, 27
    Stuttgart Radio Symphony Orchestra
      2, 27
    Theaterhaus 131
Swallow, Steve 104–5, 108, 111, 118, 122
SWF broadcasting 68

television cameras 12
Thigpen, Ed 52–53
Thompson, Barbara 131, **134**
T On a White Horse 96–97
Torn, David 125, **144**
Towner, Ralph 13, 98, 102, 115–16
    Solstice 102
    Sound and Shadows 102
Trout, Ross, 125

United Jazz + Rock Ensemble 76, 122,
    130–31, **134**, 137, 160
    Live in Schützenhaus 133
USSR 49
Uzès, France 2

Van Damme, Art 72
Van Rooyen, Ack 96, 107, 131, **134**
Van't Hof, Jasper 85, 150
Vienna 146–47
Vitous, Miroslav 111
Von Schlippenbach, Alexander 59, 62, 69

Wagenseil, Adolf 40, **41**
Wagner, Richard 27
Walcott, Collin 116, 137
Washington D.C.
    Blues Alley 110
WDR (West German Broadcasting) 12

Weber, Eberhard **6**, **20**, **30**, 37, **47**, **48**, **50**, **51**, **61**, **65**, **73**, **83**, **89**, **94**, **95**, **103**, **107**, **113**, **121**, **123**, **132**, **134**, **136**, **144**, **155**, **169**
  amplification 58, 158–61
  Artist of Year (1975) 97
  carnets for instruments 141
  cello 63
  composing 91
  electric bass 57, 158
  film work 46, **47**
  first professional gig 39–40, **41**
  five-string bass 55–56
  home in France 13
  left-hand motor skill 1, 3, 5
  stroke, 5, 13, 161, 167–169
  US visits 105, 108–110, 115–19, 142, 144–45
Weber, Gisela (Schauble, sister) 18–19, 21, 23, **30**, 46

Weber, Hans "Pipin" (father) 17–21, 25, 29, **30**, 45, 80–82, 165
Weber, Hilde (mother) 19, 20, 28–29, **30**, 45
Weber, Maja (wife) 78, 80, **81**, **82**, 84–85, 90, 95–96, 99, 111, 138
  artwork of **88**, 89–90
Weber, Reto 2
Weather Report 111
Wehner, Gerhard 50–51
Wendland, Götz 49
Wheeler, Kenny 131, **134**
Wiesbaden 85, 91, 97
Winkler, Rolf 46
Witte, Peter "Fifi" 43–44
Wittich, Roland, 21, 41, **48**, 63–64

Yellow Fields 91, 109, 114

Zawinul, Joe 111

www.ingramcontent.com/pod-product-compliance
Lightning Source LLC
Chambersburg PA
CBHW070444100426
42812CB00004B/1201